CAMBRIDGE
UNIVERSITY PRESS

CAMBRIDGE ENGLISH
Language Assessment
Part of the University of Cambridge

Cambridge English

CAMBRIDGE
OFFICIAL
PREPARATION MATERIAL

EXAM
BOOSTER
WITH ANSWER KEY

FOR ADVANCED

T0306684

Self-study edition

Carole Allsop, Mark Little and Anne Robinson

Cambridge University Press

www.cambridge.org/elt

Cambridge Assessment English

www.cambridgeenglish.org

Information on this title: www.cambridge.org/9781108564670

First published 2018

20 19 18 17 16 15 14 13 12 11 10 9 8

Printed in Great Britain by CPI Group (UK) Ltd, Croydon CRO 4YY

A catalogue record for this publication is available from the British Library

ISBN 978-1-108-56467-0

Additional resources for this publication at www.cambridge.org/advancedbooster

The publishers have no responsibility for the persistence or accuracy of URLs for external or third-party internet websites referred to in this publication, and do not guarantee that any content on such websites is, or will remain, accurate or appropriate. Information regarding prices, travel timetables, and other factual information given in this work is correct at the time of first printing but the publishers do not guarantee the accuracy of such information thereafter.

CONTENTS

MAP OF THE BOOK AND EXAM OVERVIEW

Paper 1: Reading and Use of English 1 hour 30 minutes	Worksheet 1	Worksheet 2	Worksheet 3
Part 1 p12 4-option multiple-choice cloze 8 questions / 8 marks	**Music and the arts** Collocations Review of present tenses	**Human behaviour** Verb + adjective Commonly confused adjectives Verb patterns (verb + reflexive pronoun + *each other / one another*)	**Current affairs** Research and investigation vocabulary Noun + preposition
Part 2 p18 Open cloze 8 questions / 8 marks	**Money and finance** Phrasal verbs with *come* Separable and inseparable phrasal verbs	**Science** Fixed phrase linkers Articles	**Nature and the environment** Compound nouns Dependent prepositions
Part 3 p24 Word formation 8 questions / 8 marks	**Education and learning** Prefixes Relative clauses	**Health and sport** Suffixes Participle clauses	**Travel** Gradable adjectives Word building
Part 4 p30 Key word transformation 6 questions / 12 marks	**Relationships** Expressions with *no* Inversions	**The media** Idioms Adverb positions	**The environment** Three-part phrasal verbs Cleft sentences
Part 5 p36 4-option multiple choice 6 questions / 12 marks	**Health and sport** *-ing* v *to* infinitive	**Cities and transport** Passive tenses (1)	**Technology in schools** Perfect tenses (1)
Part 6 p42 Cross-text multiple matching 4 questions / 8 marks	**Work and business** Verb + 2 objects	**The environment** *as, enough, result, so, such, too*	**Behaviour** Adjectives plus prepositions
Part 7 p48 Gapped text 6 questions / 12 marks	**Business and consumers** Perfect tenses (2)	**Technology** Nominalisation	**Arts and education** *have* or *get* + (something) + the past participle
Part 8 p54 Multiple matching 10 questions / 10 marks	**Work and training** Conditionals	**The media** Meanings of *get*	**Travel and tourism** *Do, make, have, give* and *take*

Paper 2: Writing
1 hour 30 minutes

	Worksheet 1	Worksheet 2	Worksheet 3
Part 1 p60 Writing an essay 1 question / 20 marks	**Health and sport** Words with similar meaning Contrasting linkers	**Education, learning and work** Giving opinions Conceding (*yet, whatever, whichever*)	**Community** Adverbs (*admittedly apparently, fortunately*) Rephrasing

	Worksheet 1	Worksheet 2
Part 2 p66 Writing a letter or email, a proposal, a report or a review 1 question from a choice of 3 / 20 marks	**Arts and entertainment** Adjectives praising and criticising Addition linkers	**Science** Purpose linkers (*so, so that, so as, in order to*, etc.) Fixed expressions of certainty

	Worksheet 3	Worksheet 4
	Work Formal v informal fixed expressions for writing letters	**Travel** Travel vocabulary Result linkers (*consequently, for that reason*, etc.)

Paper 3: Listening 40 minutes

	Worksheet 1	Worksheet 2	Worksheet 3
Part 1 p74 3-option multiple choice 6 questions / 6 marks	**Arts and literature** Reporting verbs Expressing opinions	**Human behaviour** Adverbs of emotion Reported speech	**Travel** Expressing purpose Modals (including passive and continuous)
Part 2 p80 Sentence completion 8 questions / 8 marks	**Science** Spelling Determiners	**Volunteering** Quantifiers Word building	**Biography** Collocations Review of past tenses
Part 3 p86 4-option multiple choice 6 questions / 6 marks	**Work and money** Reporting verbs Word order in sentences	**Health and sport** Phrasal verbs Conditionals (3rd and mixed)	**Brain and senses** Adjective and adverbials expression certainty *One / ones, either / neither, so do I / do so, too*
Part 4 p92 Multiple matching 10 questions / 10 marks	**The environment** Verb + preposition Fixed phrases	**Entertainment** Wishes and regrets Personality vocabulary	**Events and issues** Report vocabulary Conditional expressions

Paper 4: Speaking 15 minutes

	Worksheet 1	Worksheet 2	Worksheet 3
Part 1 p98 Short conversation with examiner / 2 minutes	**Education and learning** Easily confused words Talking about preferences	**Arts and entertainment** Idioms Future forms	**Travel** Frequently confused words Speculating
Part 2 p104 Comparing 2 out of 3 photographs / 4 minutes	**Health and sport** Compound adjectives Making comparisons	**Events and issues** Comparative expressions Collocations	**Human creativity** Modals for deduction
Parts 3 and 4 p110 Discussion and decision making task / 4 minutes Further discussion / 5 minutes	**Psychology** Psychological condition vocabulary Giving examples	**The environment** Clarifying / hedging Giving opinions	**Work** Negotiating Summing up

Think about it p116

Answer key p125

HOW TO USE THE EXAM BOOSTER

Welcome to the Cambridge English BOOSTER

What is the Exam Booster?

The Exam Booster provides focused exam practice of all parts of the *Cambridge English: Advanced* exam. Prepare for the exam, ensuring you gain the confidence, skills and knowledge you need for exam day.

How can I use it?

- Pick and choose the areas you want to practise at any time
- Use alongside a coursebook or on its own
- Download the audio to your computer or device – Go to www.cambridge.org/advancedbooster

How is it structured?

The Exam Booster contains 17 sections which follow the order of the exam and cover all the parts: Reading and Use of English Parts 1–8, Writing Parts 1–2, Listening Parts 1–4 and Speaking Parts 1–4.

Check exam paper, exam part and worksheet number at the top of each section.

Cover a variety of topics from the exam. Topics are suitable for *Cambridge English: Advanced* preparation.

Go to www.cambridge.org/advancedbooster to download the audio to your computer or device.

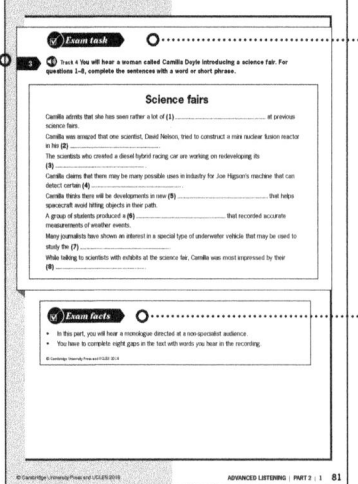

Find exam tasks easily. There are three worksheets for each exam part.

Exam facts offer clear, concise information about the exercise type and number of questions.

What other features are there?

Practise vocabulary, grammar or functional language tested in the exam using the additional tasks on the worksheet.

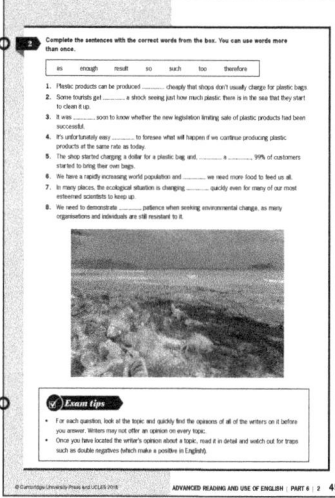

Exam tips provide practical strategies and advice on how to approach the task.

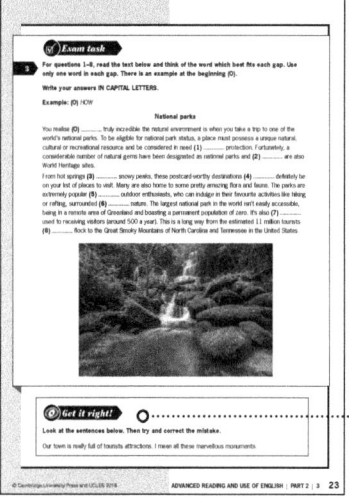

Avoid the most typical mistakes that candidates make with *Get it right!* Identify and correct common errors made by *Cambridge English: Advanced* candidates.

Use *Think about it* sections to check you understand what you need to do for each part of the exam – great either before or after attempting an exercise.

Access a complete Answer key with sample answers for the writing tasks and Audioscripts.

EXAM OVERVIEW

Paper 1: Reading and Use of English 1 hour 30 minutes

Reading and Use of English

Part	Number of questions	Number of marks	Task type	Task format
1	8	8	Multiple-choice cloze	A text in which there are eight gaps for missing words or phrases. Candidates have to chose the correct option (A, B, C or D) to fill each gap.
2	8	8	Open cloze	A text in which there are eight missing words. Candidates have to think of the correct word to fill each gap.
3	8	8	Word formation	A text in which there are eight gaps. Candidates have to change a prompt word to form the correct missing word that fills each gap.
4	6	12	Key word transformation	Six pairs of sentences. Candidates have to complete the second sentence in each pair, using a given key word, so that it has the same meaning as the first sentence.
5	6	12	Multiple choice	A text with six multiple-choice questions. Candidates have to decide which option (A, B, C or D) is the correct answer to each question.
6	4	8	Cross-text multiple matching	Four texts on a related topic. Candidates match four prompts to elements in the text to decide the correct answers.
7	6	12	Gapped text	A text in which there are six gaps and a list of seven paragraphs. Candidates have to choose the correct paragraph to fill each gap.
8	10	10	Multiple matching	A long text or several short texts and ten statements. For each statement, candidates have to decide which part of the text contains the information mentioned.
Total	56	78		

Paper 2: Writing 1 hour 30 mins

Writing

Part	Number of questions	Number of marks	Task type	Task format
1	1	20	An essay	Candidates are given an essay title and notes. They must write an essay of 220–260 words using the notes provided.
2	1 from a choice of tasks	20	An email/letter, a report / proposal, or a review	Candidates write 220–260 words, answer the question of their choosing in the way specified.
Total	2	40		

Paper 3: Listening 🔊

About 40 mins

Part	Number of questions	Number of marks	Task type	Task format
1	6	6	Multiple choice	Three short conversations. Candidates have to decide which option (A, B or C) is the answer to two questions about each conversation.
2	8	8	Sentence completion	A monologue. Candidates complete eight sentences using words from the recording.
3	6	6	Multiple matching	A conversation. Candidates answer six multiple choice questions by choosing the correct option (A, B, C or D).
4	10	10	Multiple choice	Five short monologues. Candidates have to match eight statements (A–H) in Task 1 and Task 2 to each speaker. There are three statements in each task that candidates don't need.
Total	30	30		

Paper 4: Speaking 💬

About 15 mins

Part	Timing	Interaction	Task type	Task format
1	Two minutes	Examiner ↓ Candidate	Interview	The examiner asks the candidates questions about themselves. They may be asked to talk about past experiences, present circumstances and future plans.
2	Four minutes	Candidate long turn	Long turn	Each candidate has to talk about and compare two colour photographs (out of a choice of three) without interruption. They also have to answer a short question about the other candidate's photographs.
3	Four minutes	Candidate ⤫ Candidate	Collaborative task	The examiner gives the candidates a question and some written prompts. The candidates discuss these together for minutes. The examiner will then ask them to make a decision together about the topic they have been discussing.
4	Five minutes	Candidate ⤫ Candidate	Discussion	Further discussion between the candidates, guided by questions from the examiner, about the same topic as the task in Part 3.
Total		30		

Cambridge English

The Cambridge English Scale explained

A guide to converting *Cambridge English: Advanced* practice test scores to Cambridge English Scale scores

Common European Framework of Reference (CEFR) | Cambridge English Scale | Cambridge English: Advanced

Cambridge English: Advanced is now reporting results on the Cambridge English Scale. For this exam, candidates receive an individual score for each of the four skills – reading, writing, listening, speaking – and Use of English. In the live exam, each of the skills and Use of English are equally weighted, and a candidate's overall score is calculated by adding all of the individual scores together and dividing by five (and then rounding to the nearest whole number). A candidate's grade and CEFR level are based on their performance across the whole test, and there is no requirement to achieve a minimum score in each paper.

The following tables can be used as guidance to help you convert practice test scores to Cambridge English Scale scores.

Please note that these only apply when using official Cambridge English practice tests.

The conversion tables are only intended as a guide for your readiness to take the exam. Your scores may not always reflect the results you may achieve in the live exam. They should not be used to try to predict precise scores in the live exam, but can be a useful diagnostic tool, indicating areas of relative strength and weakness.

The scores needed on any given test to achieve the scores on the Cambridge English Scale shown in the tables below will vary due to a number of factors, so scores close to CEFR boundaries need to be reviewed carefully. We recommend that this is approximately three Cambridge English Scale score points above and below the score needed to achieve the level, e.g. 177–183 for Level C1. Students who achieve only slightly higher than the Cambridge English Scale score for a given level on a practice test may not achieve that level in the live exam, and we recommend that they continue working to improve so that they reach the desired level.

Cambridge English
Advanced

Reading

The Reading section consists of Parts 1, 5, 6, 7 and 8 of the Reading and Use of English paper. Correct answers in Parts 1 and 8 are worth 1 mark each. Correct answers in Parts 5, 6 and 7 are worth 2 marks each. There are 50 possible marks in the Reading section.

Practice test score	Cambridge English Scale score	CEFR Level
43	200	C2
32	180	C1
23	160	B2
17	142*	-

*minimum score reported for *Advanced*

Use of English

The Use of English section consists of Parts 2, 3 and 4 of the Reading and Use of English paper. Correct answers in Parts 2 and 3 are worth 1 mark each. In Part 4, answers which are partly correct receive 1 mark and answers which are completely correct receive 2 marks. There are 28 possible marks in the Use of English section.

Practice test score	Cambridge English Scale score	CEFR Level
23	200	C2
16	180	C1
11	160	B2
8	142*	-

*minimum score reported for *Advanced*

Writing

Candidates' answers in the Writing paper are marked by trained examiners who are certificated to mark at the level. Answers are marked using assessment scales which are linked to the Common European Framework of Reference. 0–5 marks are given for each of the following criteria: Content; Communicative Achievement; Organisation; and Language. Whole marks only are awarded; there are no half marks given. Marks for each of the criteria are combined to give 20 possible marks for each question. There are 40 possible marks for the whole paper.

Practice test score	Cambridge English Scale score	CEFR Level
34	200	C2
24	180	C1
16	160	B2
10	142*	-

*minimum score reported for *Advanced*

Listening

Correct answers in the Listening paper are worth 1 mark each. There are 30 possible marks in the Listening paper.

Practice test score	Cambridge English Scale score	CEFR Level
26	200	C2
18	180	C1
13	160	B2
11	142*	-

*minimum score reported for *Advanced*

Speaking

Candidates take the test in pairs, but are assessed on their individual performance by trained examiners certificated to examine at the level. Candidate speaking performances are assessed using scales which are linked to the Common European Framework of Reference. The assessor gives 0–5 marks for each of the following criteria: Grammatical Resource; Lexical Resource; Discourse Management; Pronunciation; and Interactive Communication. Marks for each of these criteria are doubled. The interlocutor gives a mark of 0–5 for Global Achievement. This mark is then multiplied by five. Examiners may award half marks. Marks for all criteria are then combined, meaning there are 75 marks available in the Speaking test.

Practice test score	Cambridge English Scale score	CEFR Level
66	200	C2
45	180	C1
30	160	B2
17	142*	-

*minimum score reported for *Advanced*

CAMBRIDGE ENGLISH
Language Assessment
Part of the University of Cambridge

Converting *Cambridge English: Advanced*
practice test scores to Cambridge English Scale scores

Music and the arts

1 Complete the sentences with the correct words from the box.

bill	camera	choir	compilation	exhibition	orchestra	skills	stage

1. The composer himself is conducting the .... They are also playing works from Broadway musicals.

2. Unfortunately, the leading actor is ill, so he is not appearing on .... tonight.

3. A .... of their greatest hits is being released later this month.

4. The gallery is mounting a new .... of her lifelong works.

5. I love singing, so I'm thinking of joining a .... as soon as I can.

6. Top chefs and bakers are showing off their culinary .... and members of the public are invited to try the dishes.

7. The legendary musician tops the .... at the festival and will not disappoint.

8. The whole event is being captured on .... and will be made into a documentary.

2 Complete the sentences with the correct form of the verbs (present simple or present continuous) from the box. Sometimes, both tenses may be possible.

be (×2)	book	give	head	hit	kick	make	rest	stay	take

Indeed, these **(1)** .... busy times for us right now. We **(2)** .... three performances at the opera house this week, and they **(3)** .... all sold-out. As you know, we **(4)** .... at the Central Hotel again. Our agent always **(5)** .... our rooms here because they **(6)** .... such good care of us. Next week, we **(7)** .... for Paris, where our fans always **(8)** .... us feel so welcome. Our gigs at the French venue **(9)** .... off on Monday 28th at 9 p.m. After that, we **(10)** .... for three weeks before we **(11)** .... the road again.

Which items can you use the present simple for?

☑ Exam facts

- In this part, you read a text with eight gaps.
- You have to choose the correct word (A, B, C or D) for each gap.

3 For questions 1–8, read the text below and decide which answer (A, B, C or D) best fits each gap. There is an example at the beginning. (0)

Example:

0 **A** time   **B** season   **C** series   **D** episode
Example answer: *B*

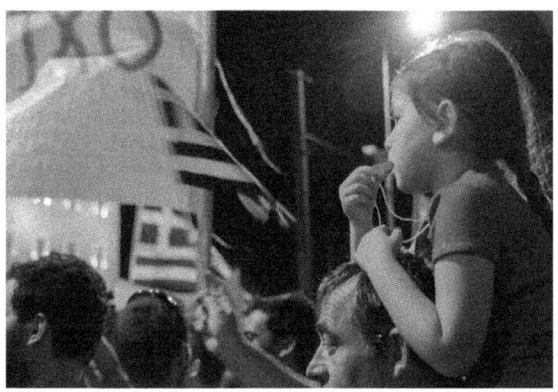

Don't miss the event of the year!

Now in its seventh **(0)** .... , this year, the Rogers Estate Festival starts a day earlier: on Thursday, which means visitors have a whole extra day to enjoy it. This showcase of art and music takes place in a **(1)** .... like no other, with the castle ruins in the background. This year's line-up includes an array of talented actors alongside a very **(2)** .... selection of both local and international musicians and visual artists.

Visitors can take **(3)** .... an impressive range of exhibits and experience both the permanent and **(4)** .... collections through their five senses. In addition to large-audience sessions, there will be more intimate moments, including poetry recitals, **(5)** .... by soloists plus painters and sculptors at work. Last but not least, on Friday, we are in for a special **(6)** .... Belinda Wilde, our guest of honour this year, is **(7)** .... her debut at the festival, giving us a preview of a new **(8)** .... of her famous symphony. If you still haven't bought your pass to the festival, what are you waiting for?

1	**A** scenery	**B** set	**C** setting	**D** stage
2	**A** supreme	**B** high	**C** luxury	**D** elite
3	**A** off	**B** up	**C** in	**D** on
4	**A** provisional	**B** temporary	**C** casual	**D** momentary
5	**A** performances	**B** productions	**C** acts	**D** presentations
6	**A** joy	**B** bliss	**C** treat	**D** treatment
7	**A** giving	**B** making	**C** taking	**D** doing
8	**A** constitution	**B** distribution	**C** organisation	**D** arrangement

Human behaviour

☑ *Exam task*

1 For questions 1–8, read the text below and decide which answer (A, B, C or D) best fits each gap. There is an example at the beginning. (0)

Example:

0 A fancy **B** inclined **C** tempting **D** dreamy

Example answer: *B*

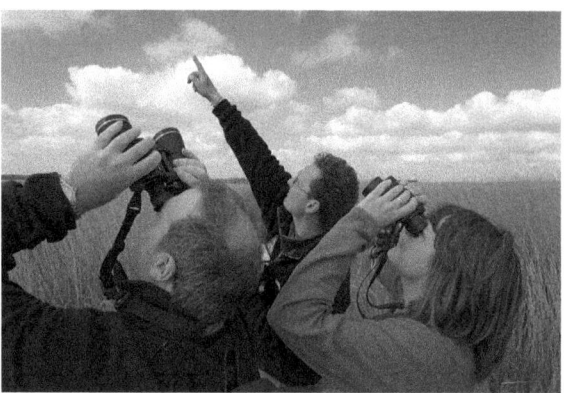

Hobbyists around the world unite

No doubt you may be **(0)** .... to think that in this day and age, traditional pursuits are no longer 'in' and that we would have **(1)** .... away with old-fashioned hobbies that don't involve computers. Nothing of the **(2)** .... If anything, the internet has made it easier for people with specialist hobbies in different corners of the planet to **(3)** .... themselves to their passion and to support one another. With one quick press of a key, **(4)** .... car collectors are online, comparing notes and restoration **(5)** .... with enthusiasts in distant lands. If a part needs replacing, a vast electronic inventory is out there **(6)** .... and waiting. After a day in the field, birdwatchers can post sightings they consider worth sharing with likeminded enthusiasts who will immediately **(7)** .... to their passion.

Thankfully, face to face contact does still take place. Historic car rallies and races have a large following. Come Sunday morning, children and adults alike still meet to swap, or perhaps even **(8)** .... , the cards missing from their collections.

1	**A** done	**B** taken	**C** put	**D** sent
2	**A** type	**B** sort	**C** variety	**D** brand
3	**A** focus	**B** present	**C** stick	**D** devote
4	**A** ancient	**B** historical	**C** classic	**D** epic
5	**A** means	**B** techniques	**C** crafts	**D** systems
6	**A** handy	**B** willing	**C** ready	**D** open
7	**A** relate	**B** share	**C** connect	**D** join
8	**A** bid	**B** purchase	**C** invest	**D** subscribe

☑ *Exam tips*

- Read through the whole text first for overall meaning.
- Read again and look at the words before and after the gaps in the text and check for clues like determiners (*that*, *this*, etc.), verb forms, pronouns and prepositions. These words may be the reason why one particular option is the correct word for the gap.

2 Complete the sentences with the correct form of a verb from the first box and an adjective from the second to form common expressions.

call	consider	find	keep	make

busy	happy	fortunate	perfect	tricky

1. You might .... it .... to choose a flatmate. You can't always rely on first impressions.
2. It would .... me so .... if you came to visit!
3. He .... himself very .... to still have a job.
4. She .... him .... all afternoon with a mountain of paperwork.
5. It's okay, but I wouldn't .... it .... There are better films.

3 Complete the sentences with the correct adjective in each gap.

1. *last / latest / previous*

   Her .... show of disrespect was to ignore me completely. .... time, she hung up the phone and on a .... occasion, she shut the door in my face.

2. *common / normal / regular*

   Why don't you use your .... sense, on a .... basis, like a .... person?

3. *big / long / wide*

   We still have a .... way to go! There's a .... difference between short-term and long-term success. At the moment, we don't have the .... experience of dealing with customers which we need.

4. *great / large / significant*

   There was .... disagreement among a .... number of members who showed .... concern about the running of the club.

5. *distant / far / remote*

   In the not too .... future, experts predict that it will be impossible to holiday .... from civilization, but for now, there are still some places on the planet that are virtually impossible to reach because they are so .... and inaccessible.

6. *different / unique / varied*

   Many .... customers have submitted reviews praising the .... location of the restaurant and the .... menu.

4 Complete the sentences with the correct form of the verbs from the box to form common expressions.

convince	express	introduce	know	learn	talk	treat

1. Please .... among yourselves for a moment while I finish setting up.
2. Living under the same roof, different generations can .... a lot from each other.
3. He's trying to .... himself that he's capable of doing it.
4. Work in groups. Please start by .... yourselves to one another.
5. She finds it extremely hard to .... herself when she's nervous and often stutters.
6. The two friends .... themselves to a spa day last week.
7. Over lunch, participants had the chance to get to .... each other a little better.

Current affairs

1 **Choose the correct preposition to complete the sentences.**

1. The campaign is not making an impact *in / on / to* voters.
2. The government is unlikely to give in to the calls *for / of / on* a referendum.
3. Thousands of workers took part in a protest *against / to / with* pay cuts.
4. The press showed no regard *at / for / on* his privacy.
5. The campaigners received little support *for / on / towards* their proposals.
6. The company has reported a record-breaking increase *in / of / up* sales.
7. Has the committee considered the consequences *for / of / on* the changes on members?
8. Several players have expressed their desire *for / of / to* leave the club next season.

2 **Complete the sentences with the correct words from the boxes.**

cases	examples	incidents	occasions

1. The company was accused of unfair use of personal data on a number of ....
2. Serious .... of passenger misbehaviour include refusing to fasten their seatbelts and trying to open the plane door mid-flight.
3. As many as a hundred people are thought to have been injured, in some .... , seriously.
4. Obvious .... of internet crimes are hacking, spreading viruses and piracy.

enquiry	investigation	research	survey

5. The cause of the fire is currently under ....
6. University scientists are carrying out .... into the side-effects of these drugs.
7. The authorities are conducting a .... of residents' thoughts on the proposed changes.
8. The government has ordered a public .... to determine the reasons for the unrest.

attention	attraction	interest	focus

9. At the core of the city is its castle, which is the main tourist ....
10. The press has now turned its .... to other matters.
11. The media .... on politicians' private lives means that many of the real, important issues are not dealt with.
12. Readers have lost .... in the story.

☑ **Exam task**

3 For questions 1–8, read the text below and decide which answer (A, B, C or D) best fits each gap. There is an example at the beginning. (0)

Example:

0 A growing **B** evolving **C** moving **D** rising

Example answer: *B*

News sharing

The way we obtain our news coverage is always **(0)** .... The public can gain information on current events from a wide variety of **(1)** .... Centuries ago, news was obtained either by word of mouth, with town criers **(2)** .... citizens of news and by-laws, or from print, with notices posted on doors of the local inn. With the **(3)** .... of radio, whole families could **(4)** .... together in the living room to listen to the daily news bulletin. Even today, when TV sets occupy a prime **(5)** .... in the most used rooms in our house, some listeners remain faithful to their radio stations. Except, of course, for the fact that many will **(6)** .... in to them on their computer or tablet instead of turning their radio dial. With the **(7)** .... use of social media, news travels faster than ever before. Minute-by-minute coverage of the news no longer relies on TV networks. Increased internet access enables individuals to share photos, opinions and even live videos with one sharp **(8)** .... on the screen.

1	**A** opportunities	**B** causes	**C** ways	**D** sources
2	**A** explaining	**B** informing	**C** noting	**D** communicating
3	**A** arrival	**B** entrance	**C** starting	**D** approach
4	**A** team	**B** gang	**C** gather	**D** unite
5	**A** area	**B** site	**C** position	**D** point
6	**A** turn	**B** switch	**C** tune	**D** start
7	**A** sweeping	**B** absolute	**C** large	**D** widespread
8	**A** stroke	**B** tap	**C** squeeze	**D** nudge

 Get it right!

Look at the sentence below. Then try to correct it.

For most of people it seems to be so natural – animals in cages.

Money and finance

1 **Complete each sentence with the correct form of *come* and the correct word from the box.**

across	between	down	into	off	through	under	up

1. The family .... a large amount of money when their grandmother passed away.
2. The company has seen some tough times, but has always .... them.
3. The minister has .... a lot of pressure to resign after the budget cuts.
4. The scheme will never .... It's just not feasible.
5. An opportunity to sell at this price may never .... again, so make the most of it.
6. I .... a pile of old bank statements in the filing cabinets.
7. The business partners vowed that nothing would .... them and that the company would survive.
8. Inflation is .... at last. The economy might recover soon.

2 **Read each pair of sentences and cross out any sentence which is wrong. Both sentences may be correct.**

1. **a** The government has put together a rescue plan to save the economy.
   b The government has put a rescue plan together to save the economy.
2. **a** I had put money aside for a rainy day, so we used that.
   b I had put aside money for a rainy day, so we used that.
3. **a** It's very difficult to live on my salary.
   b It's very difficult to live my salary on.
4. **a** We've gone through some tough times, but things will start to pick up again.
   b We've gone some tough times through, but things will start to pick up again.
5. **a** It took us eight years to pay off the debt.
   b It took us eight years to pay the debt off.
6. **a** They are bringing down interest rates again.
   b They are bringing interest rates down again.
7. **a** I'll pay you back as soon as I get paid.
   b I'll pay back you as soon as I get paid.
8. **a** The financial adviser warned that businesses should not rush the deal into.
   b The financial adviser warned that businesses should not rush into the deal.

✓ Exam task

3

For questions 1–8, read the text below and think of the word which best fits each gap. Use only one word in each gap.
There is an example at the beginning (0).

Write your answers IN CAPITAL LETTERS.

Example: (0) *WITH*

We're all in this together

Have you, or has someone you know, come up **(0)** .... an original idea for a brilliant product or an original invention? But do you find **(1)** .... without sufficient cash to develop or promote it? Fear not. Help is close **(2)** .... hand. You can crowdfund it! Crowdfunding is the practice of financing a project by raising money through contributions **(3)** .... individuals or groups of people with money to invest or the desire to **(4)** .... good. It has emerged as an accessible option for entrepreneurs and creatives around the world. Usually collected via online platforms, the sum generated allows them to both **(5)** .... their ideas to the test and gain exposure and funds for their product or invention. You might well wonder **(6)** .... crowdfunding really is a modern-day practice. It would seem **(7)** .... Although the term and its definition were only recently added to dictionaries, throughout history, landmark expeditions, epic voyages and even national monuments have been completed **(8)** .... to the donations of ordinary people.

✓ Exam facts

- In this part, you read a text with eight gaps in it.
- You have to write a word that fits each gap based on your knowledge of the language.

Science

☑ Exam task

1 For questions 1–8, read the text below and think of the word which best fits each gap. Use only one word in each gap. There is an example at the beginning (0).

Write your answers **IN CAPITAL LETTERS.**

Example: **(0)** *IT*

What do you call a . . . ?

Let's face **(0)** .... , there are some pretty weird and wonderful entries on the list of names for living creatures. Some might give you a very clear picture of **(1)** .... to expect when you look at it! A blobfish has to be round, right? You won't find leafy sea dragons on land, **(2)** .... you? In the 18th century, science took the important step of giving species two-part Latin names, such as *Homo Sapiens*, **(3)** .... a view to allowing people around the world to communicate unambiguously. To **(4)** .... certain extent, the system, known

(5) .... 'binomial nomenclature', has done its job. Names often give a clear indication of origin (*japonica*), colour (*azurea*) or size (*nana*). On the other hand, it has produced some fun terms, to **(6)** .... the least, like *Wunderpus photgenicus* or more recently, *Heteropoda davidbowie*, apparently **(7)** .... of the singer's contribution to the arachnid world. The more you swot up **(8)** .... this fascinating subject, the more you'll learn (and chuckle), believe me! I've just discovered that there's a creature called, believe it or not, a 'fried egg jellyfish'!

☑ Exam tips

- Remember to only write one word in each gap. If you write more than one word, you will lose the mark.
- Remember that your words must fit grammatically into each gap.
- Ask yourself if the word is part of a fixed phrase which may require a preposition, an adjective or noun, for example.
- Look carefully at the words immediately before and after the gap, but you will probably also need to recognise how the missing word connects to other parts of the text.

2 Complete the sentences with the correct words from the box.

accounts	first	happens	matter	now	result	time	words

1. A signal from what might, by all .... , be a moon outside our solar system has been spotted. Astronomers will use the Hubble Space Telescope to confirm whether this is the case.

2. Archaeologists have recently made major fossil finds and, as a .... , anthropologists have been able to uncover further details regarding the decline of the Neanderthals.

3. As a .... of fact, our laboratory is on the brink of announcing a key breakthrough which is set to change everything in this field.

4. Scientists are renowned for their curiosity or, in other .... , for the drive which propels their quest for answers.

5. Whatever .... next, it is crucial that the researchers receive the necessary funding to keep the project up and running.

6. .... and foremost, safety should be considered before proceeding with the tests.

7. Driverless cars. What's next? Pilotless planes apparently. For the .... being, though, humans are still needed in the cockpit.

8. Every .... and then, while studying a particular health disorder, scientists stumble upon a cure for another condition.

3 Complete the sentences with an article (*a, an, the*) or (–) if no article is necessary.

1. Has your personal experience of studying .... science subjects at .... school been .... positive one?

2. How far would you say that .... science fulfils .... useful role in .... modern society?

3. Which discovery or invention do you think has had .... most positive effect on .... society?

4. How do you think .... medicine will develop in .... future?

5. How strict do you think .... controls on .... scientific experiments should be?

6. To what extent are .... human beings to blame for .... climate change?

7. Do you think that .... advances in .... technology will be sufficient to overcome .... problem of .... world's dwindling resources?

8. Some people say that .... more we invent, ... lazier we become.

Nature and the environment

1 Complete the sentences with a compound noun formed from a word from each of the two boxes.

coastal	endangered	global	natural	oil	rural	urban	waste

areas	development	erosion	habitats	management	species	spill	warming

1. Recent reports state that many historical cultural heritage sites are in danger of disappearing into the sea as a consequence of ....

2. After the .... from a tanker, a massive clean-up operation was launched and a group has been set up to monitor the impact on marine wildlife.

3. Many countries worldwide have witnessed the migration of millions of people from .... to cities.

4. The construction of a forest city in China is a remarkable example of sustainable .... The buildings will include offices, schools and homes covered in trees and plants.

5. Ordinary citizens are becoming key players in effective .... by making sure rubbish from homes and offices is correctly sorted before it is collected.

6. The fight against .... has received a boost after the Governor signed a bill targeting CO_2 emissions in the state.

7. Unfortunately, various factors including population growth, poaching and deforestation have a negative impact on the .... of many plants and animals.

8. Some kinds of tigers, gorillas and bears are on the list of the world's most ....

2 Complete the sentences and questions with an adjective from the first box and the correct preposition from the second box. The prepositions can be used more than once.

eligible	hostile	incompatible	lacking	open-minded	prone	restricted	untouched

about	by	for	in	on	to	with

1. Not everyone who needs funds is .... grants to help them start a business.

2. Most people are generally .... change, but a minority are .... it and try and resist it.

3. The country is .... natural disasters. There are often storms, hurricanes and floods.

4. Transport in the city centre is .... public transport or local residents' vehicles.

5. Some parts of the country are still wild and .... humans.

6. The country is .... natural resources; it has to import its energy and other necessities from other countries.

7. In some companies, long hours mean having a career is .... raising a family.

☑ Exam task

For questions 1–8, read the text below and think of the word which best fits each gap. Use only one word in each gap. There is an example at the beginning (0).

Write your answers IN CAPITAL LETTERS.

Example: (0) *HOW*

National parks

You realise **(0)** .... truly incredible the natural environment is when you take a trip to one of the world's national parks. To be eligible for national park status, a place must possess a unique natural, cultural or recreational resource and be considered in need **(1)** .... protection. Fortunately, a considerable number of natural gems have been designated as national parks and **(2)** .... are also World Heritage sites.

From hot springs **(3)** .... snowy peaks, these postcard-worthy destinations **(4)** .... definitely be on your list of places to visit. Many are also home to some pretty amazing flora and fauna. The parks are extremely popular **(5)** .... outdoor enthusiasts, who can indulge in their favourite activities like hiking or rafting, surrounded **(6)** .... nature. The largest national park in the world isn't easily accessible, being in a remote area of Greenland and boasting a permanent population of zero. It's also **(7)** .... used to receiving visitors (around 500 a year). This is a long way from the estimated 11 million tourists **(8)** .... flock to the Great Smoky Mountains of North Carolina and Tennessee in the United States.

⊙ Get it right!

Look at the sentences below. Then try and correct the mistake.

Our town is really full of tourists attractions. I mean all these marvellous monuments.

Education and learning

1 **Correct the prefixes in the words in brackets.**

1. Many of the applicants for the course were considered either .... (inmature) or lacking in relevant experience.
2. The whole programme was .... (misorganised) from start to finish. No one seemed to know who was responsible for what.
3. The professor was renowned for her .... (imconventional) teaching methods.
4. Eventually, the student was able to .... (outcome) his shyness in class and speak in public.
5. 'I will not tolerate .... (disbehaviour) in my class,' the tutor warned.
6. .... (Probooking) is extremely advisable as places are limited and will be assigned on a first-come-first-served basis.
7. The most recent training was .... (untaken) more than four years ago. Further familiarisation is urgently needed.
8. The dates of the course were .... (unconvenient) so we did not attend.

2 **Complete the text with the correct relative pronouns from the box. Decide which, if any, relative pronouns can be omitted.**

that	when	where	which	who	whose	why

Example: (0) *which*

Choosing the university **(0)** .... is right for you is not as easy as it may seem. **(1)** .... this might be the case is **(2)** .... the prospectuses make all of them seem attractive. Here are some tips to help you **(3)** .... it's your turn to decide:

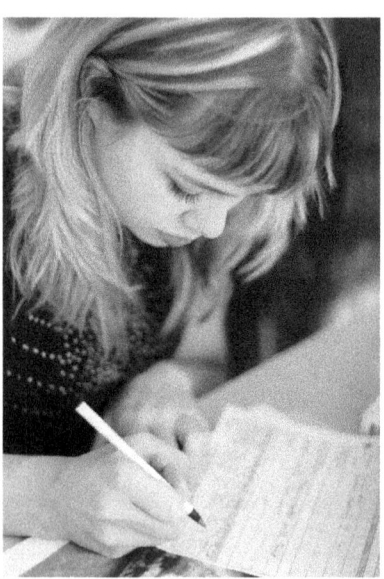

- How far is it between the halls of residence and the place **(4)** .... your lectures will take place? How will you travel around? On foot? By bike? Using public transport?
- How old are the lecturers **(5)** .... will be teaching you? Check to see if you can find any articles they've written and how recent the publication dates are.
- Read comments on student chatrooms by anyone **(6)** .... insights might prove valuable, such as undergraduates doing the same course.
- Of course, the fees **(7)** .... the university charges are a big deciding factor. Check – there may be grants available, in **(8)** .... case find out the requirements and apply.

☑ Exam task

3 For questions 1–8, read the text below. Use the word given in capitals at the end of some of the lines to form a word that fits in the gap in the same line. There is an example at the beginning (0).

Example: **(0)** *DECISION*

Making the right choice

The **(0)** .... as to which university to apply to is often   **DECIDE**
taken on the basis of a university's position on the world rankings table.
Yet, other considerations, such as whether the course is
(1) .... or offers hands-on experience and the amount of time   **THEORY**
that students will need to work **(2)** .... should be taken into account.   **DEPEND**
The fact is that some undergraduates who express their **(3)** ....   **SATISFY**
with their university experience base their **(4)** .... on poor   **COMPLAIN**
organisation, the lack of support received and on having fewer contact hours
than expected.

As higher education **(5)** .... come under increasing pressure   **PROVIDE**
to meet established targets and to maintain or improve their status, course
guidelines should **(6)** .... what participants can expect   **CLEAR**
from the course and what the course expects from them. This should
(7) .... a reduction in student drop-out rates. Inevitably, though,   **SURE**
no matter how much the content and structure is spelt out, some students will turn
up with **(8)** .... expectations that can never be met.   **REAL**

☑ Exam facts

- In this part, you read a text with eight gaps in it.
- For each gap, there is a word in capital letters at the end of the line.
- You have to form a word based on the word in capital letters to fit in the gap.

Health and sport

☑ Exam task

1 For questions 1–8, read the text below. Use the word given in capitals at the end of some of the lines to form a word that fits in the gap in the same line. There is an example at the beginning (0).

Example: (0) *PARTICULARLY*

Addressing health concerns

Healthy eating and keeping physically active are **(0)** .... important   **PARTICULAR**
for children and adolescents. Their nutrition and lifestyle have a direct impact
on their **(1)** .... and development. Moreover, worldwide trends   **GROW**
in obesity in children and teenagers are becoming **(2)** ....   **INCREASE**
worrying. Being overweight or obese has been linked to a greater
(3) .... of various health complaints later in life.   **OCCUR**

One way to improve the dietary habits of schoolchildren is to make
(4) .... to the food served for lunch. Several leading UK chefs   **ADJUST**
have launched campaigns to improve the nutritional quality of the food on school
menus. Despite **(5)** .... publicity, the improvements to school   **CONSIDER**
dinners have not really **(6)** .... Attention has now turned to   **MATERIAL**
reducing excess sugar in foods and beverages.

Some local authorities are introducing a tax on drinks with more than a permitted
amount of sugar. **(7)** .... have already begun decreasing the   **MANUFACTURE**
quantity of sugar in their drinks. Health campaigners are delighted with this
reduction and also with the news that **(8)** .... raised from the tax   **COME**
will go towards school sports.

☑ Exam tips

- Look at the words before and after each gap and decide what kind of word you need to write – for example, a noun, a verb or an adjective. If you need a noun, check whether it should be singular or plural.
- As well as adding prefixes or suffixes, check if you need to make any internal spelling changes.
- You may only need to make one change to the word given in capital letters, but most often you will have to make two or more changes.

2 Complete the sentences with nouns formed from a word in the first box and a suffix from the second box. Use each word only once.

improve	unwilling	exist	signify	exaggerate	necessary

-ance	-ence	-ity	-ment	-ion	-ness

1. Despite the campaigns by famous chefs to improve the nutritional quality of school meals, many adolescents continue to show an .... to adopt a healthy diet.

2. The huge .... of the increase in child health problems should not be underestimated.

3. It would be no .... to say that until governments took steps, soft-drink producers had done nothing to reduce the sugar content in soft drinks.

4. Health campaigners are convinced that the reduction in the sugar content of beverages will bring about a considerable .... in the current and future health of youngsters.

5. In order to tackle a problem, you first have to acknowledge its ....

6. The .... of including fresh fruit and vegetables in our everyday diet cannot be ignored.

3 For questions 1–8, rewrite the sentences so they include a present or past participle clause.

1. The judges who are considering the evidence have all got a lot of experience.
   The judges ....

2. Referees who are not giving their full attention to matches are a cause for concern.
   Referees ....

3. The sports star who is featured in the article is said to be a millionaire.
   The sports star ....

4. Gymnasts who compete in a range of events require strength, agility, flexibility and balance.
   The gymnasts ....

5. The golfer who is wearing the yellow jumper is the favourite to win the competion.
   The golfer ....

6. Anyone who wants to lose weight should diet and do exercise.
   Anyone ....

7. All the people who were selected for the experiment found it really interesting.
   All the people ....

8. Keith Jones, who underwent knee surgery less than a year ago, is not yet match-fit.
   Keith Jones ....

Travel

1a Match the adjectives in 1–7 with the pair of adjectives which have a similar, but stronger, meaning in a–g.

1. bad	a appalling, digusting
2. beautiful, impressive	b devastated, horrified
3. big	c fabulous, magnificent
4. funny	d hilarious, hysterical
5. not important or useful	e immense, enormous
6. shocked	f insane, senseless
7. stupid	g worthless, pointless

1b Use a different adjective from a–g in exercise 1a to complete each of the sentences below. More than one answer may be possible. Use each word only once.

1. The stand-up comedian on our cruise ship was absolutely .... She brought the house down.

2. It would be totally, absolutely .... not to take advantage of the discounts available for off-peak travel.

3. The latest report reveals the absolutely .... costs of building the new road structure which have overrun the original budget by millions.

4. The passengers were .... by the news that their flight had been cancelled.

5. Changing lanes in traffic congestion is utterly .... It does not save time and in fact can lead to accidents.

6. The decoration of the first-class carriages is .... No expense has been spared with the furnishings.

7. The pilot did well to land so smoothly in those .... weather conditions.

🎯 Get it right!

Look at the sentence below. Then try to correct the mistake.

Every day we learn about wrong habits we have in our daily lives and how they affect the environment.

2 ▶ **Complete each of the three sentences with a different word formed from the word in capitals.**

HAND

1. The ground staff's strike is set to continue, with accusations that the airline is totally
.... the situation.

2. First-time visitors to the area will find this guide particularly ....

3. You wouldn't guess this bike is .... The previous owner obviously looked after it.

CHANGE

4. The weather at this time of the year can be very .... , so make sure you bring a waterproof.

5. The whole area remains virtually .... , thankfully. Tourism has hardly affected it.

6. There are now several websites where travellers can .... experiences and tips.

WORK

7. Being away from home doesn't mean you have to miss out on your daily .... Our gym has everything you need.

8. Our .... staff are available 24 hours a day to help make your stay unique and memorable.

9. Thanks to great .... by the climbers, the expedition was a huge success.

☑ Exam task

3 ▶ **For questions 1–8, read the text below. Use the word given in capitals at the end of some of the lines to form a word that fits in the gap in the same line. There is an example at the beginning (0).**

Example: (0) *CHILDHOOD*

How travel inspired my life

Today, I travel all around the world as a jewellery designer, but travel was also

central to my **(0)** .... My parents encouraged my sister   **CHILD**

and me to keep records of our **(1)** .... in journals and to put   **REFLECT**

together scrapbooks with souvenirs of our adventures. Before departure, a

private tutor was hired to equip us with the **(2)** .... of our   **BASE**

destination's native tongue. My poor sister was not a **(3)** ....   **PARTICULAR**

brilliant linguist and found the whole process a considerable strain. My

experience was very different. My wanderlust was **(4)** ....   **FORCE**

when, straight out of school, I had the opportunity to spend periods in India,

Eastern Europe, Africa and Asia. I travel like a **(5)** .... explorer,   **REST**

absorbing the details of art and architecture, going into the local history and

traditions in **(6)** .... I bring this approach to my work today.   **DEEP**

I am constantly reading, researching and **(7)** .... my knowledge.   **BROAD**

Not **(8)** .... , every jewellery collection I work on is an utterly   **SURPRISE**

unique representation of a part of my life's voyage.

Relationships

1 Complete the sentences with the correct words in the box.

harm	joke	signs	surprise	thing	use	way	wonder

1. The controversy caused by his statement shows no .... of abating.
2. There's usually no .... in striking up a conversation with someone on a train, but you should keep your voice down so as not to bother other passengers.
3. When you are self-employed, there is no such .... as free time.
4. There is no .... I'm apologising to him. I've done nothing wrong.
5. It's no .... trying to tidy up. My flatmate will have the place in a mess again in no time.
6. It's no .... having to work in the same office as her. You have to watch your words all the time.
7. It came as no .... to hear that the couple were going through a bad patch, but they seem to be over it now.
8. It's no .... that you liked my neighbour. She's such good company.

2 Rewrite the sentences, starting with the expressions in brackets.

1. There was never a mention of a conflict. **AT NO POINT**

....

2. This was the first time I had come across the term 'mindfulness'. **NEVER BEFORE**

....

3. If you ever happen to see your former colleague, tell her I'm asking after her. **SHOULD YOU**

....

4. The reunion had only just begun when the fire alarm went off. **HARDLY**

....

5. In comparison to our ancestors, we eat more sugar and salt and our diet also induces more acid. **NOT ONLY**

....

6. If I'd known how stubborn my teammate could be, I would never have tried to persuade him. **HAD**

....

7. I put forward the proposal and it was accepted immediately. **NO SOONER**

....

8. Providing role models for children can inspire them to study and may also mean that they achieve more in life. **NOT ONLY**

....

Exam facts

- In this part, there are six questions.
- Each part has an initial sentence, a key word and a second sentence consisting of only the beginning and end.
- You have to complete the second sentence so it means the same as the initial sentence using the key word.

© Cambridge University Press and UCLES 2016

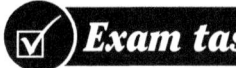 **Exam task**

3

For questions 1–6, complete the second sentence so that it has a similar meaning to the first sentence, using the word given. Do not change the word given. You must use between three and six words, including the word given. Here is an example (0).

Example:

0 The politician is not as popular now after the recession.

DECLINED

The politician's ....*popularity declined as a*........... result of the recession.

1. The changes to the club had no effect on its existing members.

CONSEQUENCE

The changes to the club .... its existing members.

2. We need to completely overhaul the terms for new users.

THOROUGH

There needs .... the terms for new users.

3. I'm absolutely certain that she was involved in the decision.

WHATSOEVER

There .... that she was involved in the decision.

4. I was never consulted, so I couldn't offer any advice on the matter.

ONCE

Never .... give my advice on the matter.

5. It's a mystery to me how he found out about the surprise party.

CLUE

I .... he found out about the surprise party.

6. The professor's reputation was such that he was nominated for the award.

REGARD

The professor was .... that he was nominated for the award.

The media

Complete the sentences with the correct words from the box.

behind	from	in	like	off	on	through	under

1. The comic is .... track to be made into the next blockbuster movie.
2. The producers of the latest fashion campaign have come .... fire from animal rights protestors.
3. I have it straight .... the horse's mouth. I spoke to an eyewitness who recorded everything.
4. The meeting will take place .... closed doors. The public won't be allowed to attend.
5. Although they say nothing in official interviews, ... the record, many people in the advertising industry admit that they are in favour of the new guidelines.
6. News that the novelist was staying at the hotel ahead of the book launch spread .... wildfire.
7. The collector heard .... the grapevine that a new, limited edition was about to be released.
8. Matthew has just put me .... the picture about what will feature in the new brochure.

Rewrite the sentences using the words given in bold. Write the sentences with the words in two positions if possible.

1. The newspaper's market share stood at 35% in the first half of the year. **APPARENTLY**

   ....

   ....

2. I was sceptical, but I think it's what the readership needed. **TO BEGIN WITH**

   ....

   ....

3. The advent of the internet hit the greeting card industry hard. **BY ALL ACCOUNTS**

   ....

   ....

4. She will pursue a career in publishing. **PROBABLY**

   ....

   ....

5. Do you think that targeted direct mail really persuades us to purchase products? **WHEN IT COMES DOWN TO IT**

   ....

   ....

6. Future issues of the magazine will be printed on recycled paper. **NEEDLESS TO SAY**

   ....

   ....

☑ *Exam task*

For questions 1–6, complete the second sentence so that it has a similar meaning to the first sentence, using the word given. Do not change the word given. You must use between three and six words, including the word given. Here is an example (0).

Example:

0   The press officer worked secretly on the campaign.

SCENES

The press officer ....*worked behind the scenes on*...... the campaign.

1.   John reads what's happening in the world on his commute to work.

DATE

John .... the news on his commute to work.

2.   Without that promotional campaign, sales would never have been so high.

FOR

If .... that promotional campaign, sales would have been lower.

3.   When it comes down to it, it's not worth the money.

AMOUNTS

What .... it is too expensive.

4.   Suddenly, the novelist became successful.

BLUE

Success .... for the novelist.

5.   I think you may be right about that the whole story being a hoax.

INCLINED

I'm .... that the whole story is a hoax.

6.   The organisers were not happy with the way the press covered the event.

ISSUE

The organisers .... of the event.

☑ *Exam tips*

- Keep your focus on the key word in your answer and don't change it in any way.
- You can use the other words in the first sentence to form the answer.
- Make sure the last word of your new phrase works with the parts of the sentence given at the beginning and end.

The environment

1 Complete each sentence with the correct expression from the box. Change the form of the verb where necessary.

> brush up on   come up against   do away with   fit in with
>   get through to   stand up to   stay away from

1. The volunteer needed to .... her Swahili before joining the fieldwork project.

2. The use of drones has .... the need for rescuers to risk their lives searching treacherous mountain ranges.

3. The decision to make the area into a nature reserve is ideal because it .... perfectly .... the conservation project.

4. Skiers have been warned to .... the area because of the risk of avalanches.

5. We need to .... the decision makers just how serious this problem is.

6. The area manages to .... pressure from ruthless developers and preserve its roots.

7. The campaign organisers have .... tremendous problems and the project has now been set back by several months.

2 Look at the sentences then rewrite each of these sentences beginning with *What* and *It's/It was*. You may need to add words.

1. The volcanic eruption forced the evacuation of hundreds of residents and the closure of the airport.
   What ....
   It was ....

2. The destruction of natural habitats causes animals to be added to the list of endangered species.
   What ....
   It's ....

3. The public response to large-scale disasters never ceases to amaze me.
   What ....
   It's ....

4. The ongoing drought has led to a ban on hose pipes for the foreseeable future.
   What ....
   It's ....

5. The roads were flooded after the torrential rain and the rivers burst their banks.
   What ....
   It was ....

6. More severe measures are needed to tackle the issue of global warming.
   What ....
   It's ....

Exam task

3

For questions 1–6, complete the second sentence so that it has a similar meaning to the first sentence, using the word given. Do not change the word given. You must use between three and six words, including the word given. Here is an example (0).

Example:

0 Some experts query the introduction of water restrictions during droughts.

SCEPTICAL

Some experts .... *are sceptical about* .... introducing water restrictions during droughts.

1. Before last Friday, representatives had not been able to reach an agreement.

UNTIL

It wasn't .... able to reach an agreement.

2. The environmentalist supported his claims with scientific evidence.

BACKED

The environmentalist's .... with scientific evidence.

3. If nothing is done to combat climate change, one tenth of the area will soon be under water.

STEPS

One tenth of the area will soon be underwater .... counteract climate change.

4. I was totally amazed at how spectacularly beautiful the coastline was.

UTTERLY

What I found .... beauty of the coastline.

5. As long as you explain your proposal clearly, they will agree.

ACROSS

If .... , they will agree.

6. Solar panels and wind turbines are far more commonplace now.

SIGHT

Solar panels and wind turbines used to .... before.

Get it right!

Look at the sentence below. Then try to correct the mistake.

I was very excited and I was looking forward for their arrival.

Exam task

1 You are going to read a review of a book about sport and philosophy. For questions 1–6, choose the answer (A, B, C or D) which you think fits best according to the text.

Knowing the score

William Skidelsky reviews David Papineau's new book, in which sport meets philosophy.

David Papineau is an eminent philosopher and a passionate lover of sport. For much of his life, he has kept the two spheres separate, fearing that to mix them would produce a double negative in his readers' appreciation of his work: philosophy robbed of its seriousness and sport of its excitement. Then, in 2012, a colleague invited him to contribute to a lecture series titled 'Philosophy and Sport', organised to coincide with that year's Olympics. 'I couldn't really refuse', Papineau recalls. 'I had an extensive knowledge of both philosophy and sport. If I wasn't going to say yes, who would?'

For his topic, he chose the role of conscious thought in fast-reaction sports, such as tennis, cricket and baseball. How, he wondered, do top tennis players like Rafael Nadal and Serena Williams use anything other than 'automatic reflexes' in the half-second (or less) they have to return their opponent's serve? How do they choose to hit the ball this way or that, to apply topspin or slice? Thinking about this not only proved 'great fun', but allowed Papineau to come away with a series of 'substantial philosophical conclusions' about the relationship between intentions and action.

After this, the floodgates were open. Having breached his self-imposed division, Papineau set about applying his philosopher's brain to a range of other sporting topics. Five years on, those inquiries have resulted in a book, *Knowing the Score*. This is essentially a collection of essays on whatever sporting questions happen to interest its author. It isn't comprehensive, nor does it advance an overarching argument. The tone – informal, anecdotal, contrarian – is more popular philosophy than academic. What unifies the book is the consistency of its approach rather than of its content: he isn't interested only in applying philosophical ideas and principles to sport. More importantly – and more originally – he wants to use arguments about sport as a launching pad into philosophy.

A good example comes in a chapter dealing with rule-breaking, in which Papineau sets off with a sporting example in order to draw parallels with broader contexts. He points out that what is acceptable in sport isn't defined by the rules alone. Sometimes it's usual to ignore them – as footballers do when they pull on opponents' shirts as the ball flies towards them. Other actions stem from a sense of fair play – such as halting the game when an opponent is lying injured – rather than arising directly from rules. Rules are just one constraint on behaviour; all sports also have codes of fair play, which operate alongside the rules, and which, in some cases, override them. Complicating matters further is the fact that official authority ultimately has a force that is greater than both. Whatever a sport's rules or codes specify, the referee or ruling body's decision is final.

Papineau argues that there's a 'remarkably close' analogy between sport's multi-level structure and the factors that constrain us in ordinary life. In sport, you can ignore the rules and still play fairly, or obey the law while being thought a cheat; similarly, in a society, citizens can break the law and still do the right thing, or comply with the law yet still indulge in objectionable behaviour. A sport's codes aren't the same as its rules; likewise, in life, we draw a distinction between virtue and legal compliance. Papineau argues that we have no general obligation to obey the law; only to do what we think is right. Yet, saying that we're not obliged to obey the law isn't the same as saying that we don't have a duty to respect the state's authority. If people didn't accept that police officers are generally entitled to tell them what to do, society might descend into chaos. Likewise, if footballers stopped listening when referees blow their whistles, the game would become a free-for-all.

Knowing the Score covers an impressive amount of ground. At a time when data analysis dominates 'serious' discussion of sport, Papineau's faith in the power of anecdote and reasoning is refreshing. The author at times gives the impression of being the sort of person who knows he's the cleverest in the room. For the most part, however, he barely puts a foot wrong in what is a blinder of a performance.

1. In the first paragraph, the reviewer suggests that Papineau

   A was in two minds whether to take on the lectures on sport and philosophy.

   B thought no one was better qualified than him to combine sport and philosophy.

   C was disappointed with previous attempts to unite sport and philosophy.

   D thought that philosophy was of greater value to people's lives than sport.

2. What does the reviewer say Papineau gained through delivering his lecture series?

   A knowledge of how 'automatic reflexes' suppress conscious thought in many situations

   B insight into the steps involved when sports stars have to make choices under pressure

   C understanding of the connections between people's aims and what they subsequently do

   D awareness of why sports stars' reactions are superior to those of ordinary people

3. What point is made about Papineau's book in the third paragraph?

   A It examines previously overlooked aspects of sport.

   B Its style is inappropriate for the subject matter.

   C It doesn't convincingly link sport and philosophy.

   D The areas of sport that it covers are very diverse.

4. What does the reviewer suggest in the fourth paragraph?

   A Breaking rules should be punished more consistently by those in power.

   B Rules play only a partial role in defining what is appropriate or inappropriate.

   C Many sportsmen and women abuse situations which lack a clear set of rules.

   D Codes of fair play carry more weight with sports stars than official rules.

5. In the fifth paragraph, the reviewer draws a comparison between behaviour in sport and

   A a broad system of morality in society.

   B a deep respect for authority in society.

   C people's tolerance of unreasonable laws.

   D society's attitudes towards rule-breakers.

6. In the final paragraph, the reviewer says that Papineau

   A uses too lightweight an approach to deal with philosophical issues.

   B relies overly on insignificant detail to support his opinions.

   C comes across as somewhat arrogant in various parts of the book.

   D chooses some poor examples to illustrate points he's making.

Choose the correct alternative to complete these sentences.

1. He started his talk by *point / to point / pointing* out that he had worked as a professional coach.

2. *To avoid / Avoid / Avoiding* injury throughout a whole career is, of course, impossible.

3. After a few years in the game, players really ought *know / to know / knowing* what is acceptable behaviour and what is not.

4. The team are so far ahead in the league that they really need not *worry / to worry / worrying* about today's result.

5. When *join / to join / joining* a new club, players always undergo a thorough medical examination.

6. Everybody was really looking forward *watching / to watch / to watching* the match.

7. If you look on the internet, you're bound *find / to find / to finding* a club near where you live.

8. Their manager didn't seem to mind me *ask / to ask / asking* him about his team's poor result.

☑ **Exam facts**

- In this part, you read a long text.
- You have to choose the correct answer (A, B, C or D) for six questions.

Cities and transport

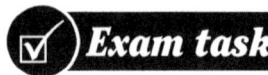

✓ Exam task

1 You are going to read an article about solving traffic problems in cities. For questions 1–6 choose the answer (A, B, C or D) which you think fits best according to the text.

Reclaiming our city streets

How two experiments could help urban dwellers reclaim their streets from traffic.

Many city-dwellers around the world face a dilemma: despite living a relatively short distance from local shops and services, a wide dual-carriageway has to be negotiated in order to get there. Whilst this poses few problems for the vast majority of people, there are those who can only make it as far as half way with each push of the pedestrian crossing button. Running out of milk has significant consequences.

In the Dutch city of Tilburg, ten people have been taking part in a trial of Crosswalk, a smartphone app that gives pedestrians with limited mobility extra crossing time. This ground-breaking experiment enables participants to cross the road in one go, without needing to dodge cars. A sensor in the traffic lights is constantly on the lookout for anyone with Crosswalk on their phone. It scans both sides of the road and adjusts the crossing time automatically, once a pedestrian carrying the app has been detected. Each user triggers a specific time which is pre-installed onto their phone and varies according to their level of mobility. In this way, delays to traffic are also minimised. The app works in combination with GPS and the software that operates the traffic lights, thus getting around the need to install further devices to control the system.

The pilot project is part of a 25-year plan to make Tilburg's road network more pedestrian and cycle-friendly. Another system under development there senses when bikes are approaching a junction and changes the lights sooner than it otherwise would, thereby giving cyclists priority over motorists. A logical extension of this technology could trigger lights to green to let ambulance or fire crews pass through. Smart traffic lights can also have environmental benefits, for example, by giving lorries a clear run through urban areas and reducing the frequency with which they have to stop and start, they thereby reduce emissions, noise pollution and damage to road surfaces. All of this
line 39 seems a far cry from the majority of urban centres.

The applications of the technology are virtually limitless and could form a major weapon in the battle to recapture city streets worldwide from motor vehicles and reduce pollution. To put this into context, in Barcelona, which is anything but large relative to many modern urban sprawls, air pollution is estimated to cause around 3,500 premature deaths per year out of a population of 1.6 million. Additionally, it is responsible for severe effects on ecosystems and agriculture. Traffic, which is the major contributor to this problem, also causes noise pollution beyond levels considered healthy. Scaling this bleak picture up for larger metropolitan areas could be bad for your health!

The World Health Organisation recommends that every city should have a minimum of 9 m^2 of green space per resident. While some places come out well relative to this figure (London scores an impressive 27, and Amsterdam an incredible 87.5), many do not. Tokyo currently has around 3 m^2 per person, and is far from alone in providing insufficient 'lungs' for its population. Picture the effect on these figures of banning traffic from the majority of a city's streets and allowing these roads to be converted into community areas, such as parks and pedestrian zones. Such a system, known as 'superblocks', is rapidly gaining support in many of the world's urban centres.

The idea has at its heart the notion that streets belong to people and not cars. Roads are repurposed within an area known as a superblock, leaving only the streets around the perimeter accessible to vehicles. Taking up less space than a neighbourhood, but larger than the blocks in many cities, their design ensures that no one would ever be more than 300 m from a road. This may mean sacrificing the parking spaces assigned to properties within them, but that's a small price to pay. By increasing the frequency of bus stops on the surrounding streets and applying smart traffic management technology as used in Tilburg, it would be possible to make public transport more effective despite having significantly fewer vehicle-accessible roads. This could be paired with a new system of cycling lanes in the areas off-limits to traffic.

Given that the majority of the world's population now lives in an urban environment, imagine the number of people who would benefit from this combination of ideas.

1. In paragraph 1, the writer is
   A offering an opinion about city life.
   B exemplifying one aspect of city life.
   C giving a reason why city life can be expensive.
   D suggesting city life is hard for most people.
2. In the second paragraph, we learn that Crosswalk
   A detects the presence of vehicles.
   B can be programmed by its users.
   C has been relatively easy to set up.
   D is being trialled on one major road.
3. What is the writer emphasising in the sentence 'All of this seems a far cry from the majority of urban centres' in line 39?
   A the contrast between aims and the current reality.
   B how upsetting living in some cities can be.
   C how advanced technology is in certain regions.
   D the technological changes happening worldwide.
4. What point does the writer make in the fourth paragraph?
   A Smaller cities have relatively high levels of pollution.

B Having farms near cities decreases harmful pollution.
C Problems caused by pollution multiply with city size.
D Embracing technology eases harmful pollution levels.

5. What does the writer suggest about green spaces in the fifth paragraph?
   A Most cities exceed international green space guidelines.
   B Modern cities have fewer green spaces than old ones.
   C Much urban green space worldwide has disappeared.
   D Many city authorities should change their green space policy.
6. According to the writer, all of the following people would benefit from the introduction of superblocks except
   A bus users.
   B residents.
   C cyclists.
   D pedestrians.

Exam tips

- Skim the text before answering the questions to get an idea of what it's about.
- When trying to identify the correct answers, try to rule out the wrong answers too.

2 In a notebook, rewrite the sentences using the passive form of the verbs so they have the same meaning as the first sentence. The number after the sentence tells you how many verbs you need to change.

1. The bus company is considering proposals to increase the number of bus routes. (1)
2. People say that it's the most cosmopolitan city on the planet. (1)
3. They told the mayor that he should create more parks. (2)
4. The city authorities will publish the results of the poll after they have counted the votes. (2)
5. They said that they couldn't do anything until they had cleared the rubbish away. (2)
6. Vandals damaged the shopping centre after they had broken into it. (2)
7. The police arrested a man after they had stopped him for driving too fast. (2)
8. Mrs Evans has asked me to inform you that she has cancelled the next residents' meeting. (2)

Technology in schools

☑ Exam task

1 You are going to read an article about using video games in education. For questions 1–6 choose the answer (A, B, C or D) which you think fits best according to the text.

Using video gaming in education

It has become conventional wisdom that spending too much time playing video games has a detrimental effect on children's studies and their social development. However, some educationalists are now questioning this theory and are using video games as effective educational tools thus bridging the gap between recreational and educational activities.

Due to the sophisticated nature of today's games, teachers are able to justify the inclusion of video and online games for many pedagogical reasons. There may, for example, be sociological, psychological, and ethical implications built into the gameplay. Harvey Edwards, who teaches IT classes in London, was one such educator who decided to use video games in his lessons. To do this, he chose Minecraft, an online game in which players create and develop imaginary worlds. He was somewhat uneasy about attempting such an unconventional approach, not because of some students' unfamiliarity with the game but rather due to them not being able to make sense of what he was trying to do with it. He worried that it might interfere with his learners' focus, but he couldn't have been more surprised by the results.

Minecraft is an example of a 'sandbox game', in which gamers roam around and change a virtual world at will. Instead of having to pass through numbered levels to reach certain places, there's full access from start to finish. The original version can be adapted to control which characters and content are left in. Each student can then be allocated tasks – such as house-building, locating items or problem-solving – which they must complete within the game. Elements of more general skills can be subtly incorporated into the lessons, such as online politeness and safety, teamwork and resolving differences. Edwards feels that presenting such lessons in the context of a game students probably already know and enjoy enables him to connect with them at greater depth, and in more motivational ways.

Bolstered by his success, Edwards introduced his approach to another school nearby. He recalls that the first couple of sessions didn't live up to his expectations. Those who had played Minecraft before were keen for others to adopt their own style of play. Unsurprisingly, this assortment of styles and opinions as to how the game should proceed were far from harmonious. However, the sessions rapidly

transformed into something more cohesive, with the learners driving the change. With minimal teacher input, they set about choosing leaders and established several teams, each with its own clearly-defined role. These teams, now party to clear common goals, willingly cooperated to ensure that their newborn world flourished, even when faced with the toughest of challenges.

'Human' inhabitants in a Minecraft 'society' are very primitive and wander around the imaginary world, waiting for guidance from players. This dynamic bears a resemblance to traditional education, an observation highlighted by Martina Williams, one of the leaders of the group. 'Through the game, we were no longer passive learners in the classroom, being told what and how to learn, but active participants in our own society.' Each group member had ideas as to how their function should develop. The leaders, meanwhile, had a vision for their virtual world as a whole, encouraging everyone to play their part in achieving the group's goals. Through creating their own characters and using these to build their own 'world', students will have gained some experiential understanding of societal structure and how communities work.

But not everyone is convinced by video games' potential academic value. While many progressive commentators cite extensive evidence to maintain that video games encourage collaboration and build problem-solving skills, more traditional factions continue to insist they are a distraction that do not merit inclusion in any curriculum. Even less evangelical cynics, who may grudgingly acknowledge games have some educational benefit, assert that this is only the case in the hands of creative educators. However, the accusation most often levelled at video games is that they detract from the social aspect of the classroom, particularly taking part in discussions. Dr Helen Conway, an educational researcher, argues that video games can be used to promote social activities. 'Students become animated talking about the game and how to improve their game-playing and problem-solving skills,' she says. 'I find it strange, this image that many people have,' Conway says. 'Children are often totally detached from their peers when undertaking more traditional activities, like reading books, but we never suggest that books are harmful because they're a solitary experience.'

1. The first time Edwards used a game in his classes, he was

   A convinced that learners would realise why he wanted them to play it.

   B convinced that learners would see the reasons for playing it.

   C anxious that he had chosen the wrong one for learners to play.

   D sure that his reasons for getting learners to play it were valid.

2. The writer suggests that Minecraft is a good choice of educational game because

   A any number of learners can use it simultaneously.

   B teachers can remove any inappropriate material.

   C gamers can create educative tasks whilst playing it.

   D players can develop their skills in a step-by-step way.

3. Which of the following words in the fourth paragraph is used to convey a feeling of approval?

   A keen

   B harmonious

   C driving

   D newborn

4. In the fifth paragraph, the writer draws a comparison between a Minecraft 'society' and

   A relationships within the group as they played.

   B the way in which countries organise themselves.

   C typical students in a school environment.

   D how leadership operates in different situations.

5. In the sixth paragraph, the writer feels that critics of video games in education

   A are unwilling to admit that using them in class has benefits.

   B make accurate observations about teachers who use them.

   C use flawed research to support their objections to using them.

   D acknowledge the drawbacks of more traditional teaching methods.

6. The words 'this image' in the sixth paragraph refer to

   A people who criticise gaming in education.

   B students discussing a game in a group.

   C a group of students reading individually.

   D a solitary player absorbed in a game.

---

2 Complete the sentences with the correct perfect tense form of the verb in brackets.

1. The video game .... more money than any other game in history. (make)

2. The company estimates that it .... more than 200,000 laptops by the end of this year. (sell)

3. The students told the teacher that they .... Minecraft many times before. (play)

4. We .... this topic for about four weeks now, and I find it really interesting. (study)

5. I .... so many different computers over the last five years, but this one is the best. (try)

6. He .... music files for about ten minutes when his computer crashed. (download)

7. Tony .... a lot of positive feedback about the new smart phone, so decided to buy it. (read)

8. At this rate, the lesson .... before we .... this software working properly. (finish, get)

 Get it right!

Look at the sentence below. Then try to correct the mistake.

Dear Alex, I am happy to receive a letter from you.

Work and business

☑ Exam task

1 You are going to read four extracts from articles in which experts give their views on progress and tradition. For questions 1–4, choose from the experts A–D. The experts may be chosen more than once.

Which expert

expresses a different view to the others about how rapid progress has affected people's happiness?	**1** ....
expresses a similar view to B about the impact of rapid progress on economic prosperity?	**2** ....
has a different view to the others about the effect of rapid progress on working life?	**3** ....
expresses a different view to C about the rise in the age at which couples have children?	**4** ....

The world we live in is changing fast – but is this a good thing?

A   Aloza Henry

A modern mythology has developed about traditional customs holding up the financial evolution of a country; it suggests that shedding them will somehow prove liberating. There's as much truth in this as in most legends. This is in contrast to the fears that many commentators raise about certain patterns closer to home, such as the average parental age for starting a family. Considering that seeking to establish a career has gained priority over committing to parenthood, I'm beginning to wonder whether our ancestors had it right. No one has ever satisfactorily explained the reason to me as to why the balance between work and home life has shifted so far towards the former. It stands to reason, however, that those who love their jobs will be more than content with this situation. On the other hand, as the majority of our workforce don't share this luxury, there can only be one outcome in terms of the population's degree of contentment.

B   Guillermo Alvarez

There are countless surveys carried out worldwide every year which monitor the satisfaction levels of different populations, and the majority of these consistently demonstrate an upward trend. I can't help but think that there's a strong correlation between these figures and the increasing levels of prosperity that most nations, and the individuals within them, have experienced. This has come about through rapid development, which has inevitably meant sacrificing some old, well-loved ways of doing things. I'm not sure many people mourn the loss of the repetitive jobs of yesteryear, but the shorter hours that went alongside them have clearly been consigned to history. As people are generally putting off starting a family far more than in previous generations, this will bring them the kind of maturity that will help to make what is a very challenging few years more fruitful as their offspring develop and grow.

C   Kasper Voss

Whilst the average employee these days probably rues the direction in which the length of their week is going, I'd be surprised if they felt the same way about its mundanity. Factory work has become increasingly mechanised, leading to an expansion in more gratifying work. Given that there are also far more diverting leisure activities to occupy us these days, it's little wonder that there's a tangibly more light-hearted mood than 30 years ago. As with all changes, there are inevitably losers as well as winners, and I'm far from convinced that having close to middle-aged parents is going to stand the newest generation in good stead. That said, by the time the first child arrives, both mother and father are generally some way up the career ladder. This is one example of the many ways in which swift development has contributed to the enhancement of many nations' wealth.

D   Zhang Wei

The rapid progress we've seen over the last few decades has been interesting to live through. Despite some notable clouds on the horizon, it has been an era which we have ended in a more comfortable and optimistic frame of mind than when we started. Most full-time employees' hours are gradually being reduced as some of what has frankly been an over-stretched and untenable workload is taken over by the rapidly increasing cohort of part-time staff. It's extremely hard to judge whether the financial situation has improved over that time for a majority of the world's population. What clouds the issue more than anything is the astonishing rise in the number of people on the planet. I've yet to be persuaded that the recent rise in starting a family later in life will spread sufficiently to control this. It's my view that starting a family when in your forties goes one step too far against nature.

---

2   **Choose the correct alternative to complete the sentences, a or b.**

1. He gave ....
    a   to his employees some advice.   b   his employees some advice.

2. Can you please explain ....
    a   this theory on development to the class?   b   the class this theory on development?

3. I'd like you to write ....
    a   to me a letter explaining the changes.   b   me a letter explaining the changes.

4. The professor asked ....
    a   the students their opinions on the trend.   b   to the students their opinions on the trend.

5. She described ....
    a   for him her family background.   b   her family background to him.

6. He took ....
    a   the report Mrs Green once it was finished.   b   Mrs Green the report once it was finished.

7. The teacher asked his colleague to ....
    a   leave him the book when she went.   b   leave the book to him when she went.

8. The company decided to offer ....
    a   staff an extra three days' holiday.   b   to staff an extra three days' holiday.

☑ **Exam facts**

- In this part, you read four texts giving different opinions on a topic.
- You must read all the texts to be able to match questions summarising opinions to the texts.

The environment

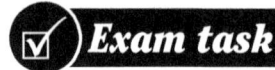 **Exam task**

1 You are going to read four extracts from articles in which experts give their views on banning single-use plastic products such as shopping bags and drinks bottles. For questions 1–4, choose from the experts A–D. The experts may be chosen more than once.

Which expert

shares B's views regarding how easy it would be to implement any ban or restrictions?	**1** ....
has a different view to the others about adding charges to the prices of single-use plastic products?	**2** ....
shares A's views on the environmental impact of imposing a ban?	**3** ....
expresses a different view to D about the economic effects of introducing a ban?	**4** ....

Banning single-use plastic products

A Doran Yusef

There has been little debate as to whether it actually makes ecological sense to ban single-use plastic products. I find this troublesome, given that the paper and glass, which would presumably replace the plastic used in bags and bottles respectively, use more energy than plastic in their production, therefore contributing more to global warming. Changing the material that these products are created from will have minimal financial impact, as income and employment losses in plastics and packaging would be absorbed into the manufacturing of whichever material takes its place. Costs imposed on consumers at the point of sale for plastic bags have been highly successful in reducing how many are used, so now is the moment to enforce these on other items packaged in disposable plastic. Any outright ban may be challenging to police and would have to be instigated gradually, in order to make it workable.

B Hideko Suzuki

Customers have little or no direct control over what packaging a company sells its products in. It's therefore unfair to inflict additional expenses on buyers for decisions made by the producer. Along similar lines, if shops want to sell their goods, they should provide and pay for the means of carrying it home. I think the financial implications of a ban on the products are more far-reaching than anyone has predicted. You can't just remove an entire industry from a nation and expect no repercussions. What's driving the call for a ban, of course, are the catastrophic consequences to the planet of avoiding this issue. I wholeheartedly go along with the view that it needs to be addressed, but perhaps not so quickly that we end up creating more problems than we solve. These sorts of transitions take time, especially as the regulation of such a ban is likely to be extraordinarily complex.

C Radislav Kovac

The majority of those calling for stopping short of a ban on throwaway plastics claim that it would be absurdly complicated to introduce and supervise. I would beg to differ. Is it really such an effort to visit a supermarket to see which manufacturers still use plastic packaging, and whether customers are being provided with plastic bags? There's no reason why they should be, as schemes worldwide whereby customers pay for these have been immensely effective and should now encompass other single-use products. Having said that, although plastic is undoubtedly a major pollutant, it would be wrong to completely ignore the likely impact of producing other more energy-intensive materials that might replace it. However, I believe these would be the lesser of two evils. Also, although the focus has largely been on packaging and bags, there needs to be a widening of the net to include other everyday items like drinking straws.

D Joanna Muller

Even though sustainable industries are relatively new, there are already sufficient examples where any reductions in revenue caused by the termination of a more traditional product are in effect cancelled out by the success of its replacement. That said, imposing an immediate ban on plastic bags may well be a step too far especially if it were too sudden for consumers to cope with. However, I'm all for an obligatory raising of prices worldwide for products sold in environmentally-unfriendly packaging, in effect an extension of the highly fruitful policy of making plastic bags prohibitively expensive. This pricing strategy has been generally straightforward to monitor and oversee, as spot checks on retailers can quickly establish whether or not any legislation is being followed. Another case for gradually implementing controls is that replacing plastics, which create physical pollution, with materials that produce excessive harmful emissions during their manufacture doesn't currently make sense. Greener alternatives need to be found.

2 Complete the sentences with the correct words from the box. You can use words more than once.

as	enough	result	so	such	too	therefore

1. Plastic products can be produced .... cheaply that shops don't usually charge for plastic bags.

2. Some tourists get .... a shock seeing just how much plastic there is in the sea that they start to clean it up.

3. It was .... soon to know whether the new legislation limiting sale of plastic products had been successful.

4. It's unfortunately easy .... to foresee what will happen if we continue producing plastic products at the same rate as today.

5. The shop started charging a dollar for a plastic bag and, ... a ...., 99% of customers started to bring their own bags.

6. We have a rapidly increasing world population and .... we need more food to feed us all.

7. In many places, the ecological situation is changing .... quickly even for many of our most esteemed scientists to keep up.

8. We need to demonstrate .... patience when seeking environmental change, as many organisations and individuals are still resistant to it.

☑ *Exam tips*

- For each question, look at the topic and quickly find the opinions of all of the writers on it before you answer. Writers may not offer an opinion on every topic.

- Once you have located the writer's opinion about a topic, read it in detail and watch out for traps such as double negatives (which make a positive in English!).

Behaviour

 Exam task

1 You are going to read four extracts from articles in which academics give their views on behaviour in schools. For questions 1–4, choose from the academic A–D. The academics may be chosen more than once.

Which academic

has a different view to the others about the historical trends in student behaviour?	**1** ....
expresses a similar view to B about what should be done to improve student behaviour?	**2** ....
expresses a different view to A on the broader social consequences of poor student behaviour?	**3** ....
has a similar view to B about the effect of behavioural issues on student achievement?	**4** ....

Behaviour in schools

A   Dorota Ignatieff

Student behaviour in schools is a topic that many people are anxious about these days, and rightly so. Recent surveys amongst teachers have given me most cause for concern, especially the reflections of those who have been teaching ten years or more who report a deterioration in standards of behaviour. Although there's no evidence as yet of a concurrent increase in antisocial activities outside of school among the age group, I suspect we may see this emerge in years to come. Despite this, concern about pupils' results seems to be largely unfounded, as there has been a gradual improvement in academic results over the last 20 years or so. This is quite some attainment given that, over the same period, funding for schools has fallen in real terms. This shortfall is the underlying cause of poor conduct, as support for more disruptive students has been eroded, and therefore is what those in power need to rectify.

B   Sunil Kumble

Student behaviour has been an issue for as long as schools have been in existence. Teachers have more influence over their students than anyone, so clearly filling the apparent gap in their training would achieve more than any government minister could. The usual hysterical media coverage has made it more or less impossible to ascertain the actual extent of any fluctuation in standards of student conduct, and indeed even to know which direction it has taken over time. What we can be sure of is that, in schools where behaviour is an issue, levels of attainment for learners from better-off families have fared well, while their poorer counterparts have once again lost out. It remains to be seen whether this will lead to problems in the wider world. Indicators such as petty crime levels are currently stable, but I'd anticipate a sharp rise if this is as big an issue as many suggest.

C   Ruth Iveson

Some of the means by which it used to be achieved in the past may not be particularly palatable today, but there's little doubt that over two generations, respect for authority in schools and associated standards of behaviour has suffered a steep decline. The root of the problem sits squarely on the shoulders of those who deal with students on a day-to-day basis. Qualifications for educators clearly haven't kept pace with the speed at which life in schools is changing, so this needs addressing. Although official figures show a steady fall in problems such as graffiti and vandalism, I believe the reverse to be true. They've become such commonplace occurrences now that they're seldom reported, and I can't help but feel that this is not unconnected to people becoming increasingly tolerant of disrespect in schools. Clearly this would also explain the decline in success rates that's starting to emerge. Students appear to have lost their focus on learning.

D Joao Rodrigues

When one analyses school results these days, it's always a good idea to dig a little deeper than perhaps schools or the government would want. On the surface, all appears to be well, as overall pass rates continue to rise. Nevertheless, the breakdown for how different social classes perform shows the opposite to be true for less affluent students. Behavioural difficulties in schools are evident in students from every strata of society, but clearly they affect this group more than others. Therefore, financial assistance needs to be made available for schools to better support these vulnerable learners and to help them eradicate the underlying problem. Schools simply don't have the resources to do this these days. I think it's no coincidence that, as government provision has declined, levels of misconduct have done the contrary. Teachers are generally devoted to their students yet unfairly receive much of the blame when their charges misbehave.

2 ▶ **Complete the sentences with an adjective and preposition. Use one word from each box.**

astonished	capable	famous	furious	involved	keen	opposed	worried

about	by	for	in	of	on	to	with

1. Only a handful of schools are truly .... their excellent standards of behaviour and achievement.

2. Many school pupils are .... much better behaviour than they actually display.

3. If students feel that they are .... making decisions that affect their lives at the school, behaviour generally improves.

4. Many people are .... school uniforms, but others believe they improve standards of behaviour.

5. There's no need to be .... behaviour in schools – it's no worse than 50 years ago.

6. The parents were .... their daughter for always forgetting to pass on important messages to them from her teacher.

7. The school inspectors were .... the improvement in behaviour since their last visit and couldn't believe how much progress had been made.

8. The head teacher was very .... pointing out to anyone who would listen the link between bad behaviour in schools and academic achievement.

 Get it right!

Look at the sentence below. Then try to correct the mistake.

The further education sector is much bigger as opposed to the university sector in the UK.

Business and consumers

☑ Exam task

1 You are going to read a magazine article about green businesses. Six paragraphs have been removed from the article. Choose from the paragraphs A–G the one which fits each gap (1–6). There is one extra paragraph which you do not need to use.

Making profits from sustainable industry

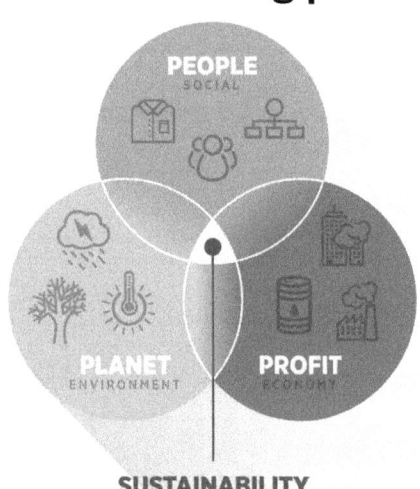

Green companies have succeeded in doing what few thought possible – making sustainability profitable.

Over the nine years I've spent trying to persuade business leaders to embrace sustainability, the question I've most often been asked is, 'What's the business case for sustainability?' This question is always delivered in a sceptical tone, carrying the unspoken suggestion that there is no business case, or at least not a very compelling one. And, for those nine years, I'd always wished I had a better answer.

| 1 |

These so-called green giants – which include electric car maker Tesla – manufacture a stunning array of goods, including burritos and beauty cream, sports shoes and organic baby food. In the process, they have succeeded in doing what the market long thought impossible: they've made sustainability profitable.

| 2 |

Despite this, it's not hard to see why so many people are surprised by the idea that a sustainable business could be profitable. In his 1970 essay, 'The Social Responsibility of Business is to Increase its Profits', American economist Milton Friedman dismissed any business with a 'social conscience' as 'unadulterated socialism'. In the following years, the notion that sustainability, or social good generally, and profit are fundamentally opposing forces hardened into fact in the minds of most business leaders.

| 3 |

For years, the conventional wisdom had been that sustainability is likely to lose a company money. Many still think that, at best, it's a strategy to reduce costs, through things like energy and water efficiency.

| 4 |

This phenomenon is also evident in companies which have diversified to produce sustainable as well as conventional brands. Many businesses, perhaps sensing a change in people's attitudes, now market environmentally-friendly products alongside their more well-established cousins. The greener products are outselling their more traditional equivalents.

| 5 |

Such a demonstration of acceptance by the capitalist establishment is profoundly important. It represents a fundamental shift and evidence that this sector of the market has long-term viability. For the green giants, sustainability is not about how they save money, but about how they make it. No longer are sustainability and profit at odds; on the contrary, rather than being a drag on profit, sustainability can drive it.

In many companies, sustainability is a department, but for the green giants, it's a value that is fully integrated into how their business is organised.

| 6 |

Together, the green giants have proven that businesses based on sustainability and social good are an extremely viable alternative to business as usual. With global climate change being taken increasingly seriously in many places around the world, close your eyes, and the pace of change will have only accelerated by the time you open them again. Ignore the green giants' example at your peril.

A This shift in consumer demand has led to a renewal of stock market interest in these more traditional firms. As is the case with the green giants, their stock market value regularly and significantly outperforms a portfolio of less forward-thinking competitors.

B Thanks to the vision of these, and other, brave entrepreneurs, they have silenced many of the doubters by collectively generating over $100 billion in annual revenue. Not only that, they do so with profit margins that are generally wider than the industry averages.

C That's why these companies thrive even though their ethical and humane raw ingredients are more expensive. Their whole cost structure has been built to accommodate these higher prices, so they still command healthy profit margins nearly three times the industry average.

D So if a product targets only a consumer niche, it's hard to make any significant revenue; there simply aren't enough people who take green values seriously enough to get you there. Green giants, however, appeal to mainstream customers or consumers.

E But while these perceived notions of it being an exercise in saving rather than making money are still widespread, they are not actually supported by the overwhelming bulk of evidence. Several green giants are actually growing faster than conventional business lines.

F There are now, however, at least nine companies globally that generate a billion dollars or more in annual revenue from products or services that have sustainability or social good at their core. They perhaps provide the evidence needed to convince even the hardest of these cynics.

G This fact is confirmed by numerous conversations I've had with professionals who promote the cause of the sustainable industry. Some are still struggling to persuade many of their business colleagues of the case for change.

---

2 Choose the correct alternative to complete the sentences.

1. Consumers *have been demanding / had been demanding* greener products for years before they finally arrived.

2. By the time the product's popularity peaks, it *would have been / will have been* on the market for about a year.

3. The 'green giants' *have traded / had traded* in this country for about six or seven years now.

4. If the trend continues, by 2020 the company's profits *will have been continuously growing / have been continuously growing* for more than ten years.

5. Traditional industry *has often considered / has often been considering* changing its organisational structure.

6. The stock market *has been rising / had been rising* for many years before the economic crash happened.

7. Scientists *had invented / might have invented* more efficient batteries if there *has been / had been* more funding.

8. If more money *has been invested / had been invested* in their development, low-energy lights *would have been developed / have been developed* much sooner.

☑ **Exam facts**

- In this part, there is one long-gapped text which has six paragraphs removed and placed in a different order after the text, with an additional seventh paragraph to distract the reader.
- You have to decide which are the six correct paragraphs and where they go in the main text.

© Cambridge University Press and UCLES 2016

Technology

 Exam task

1 You are going to read a magazine article about microwave ovens. Six paragraphs have been removed from the article. Choose from the paragraphs A–G the one which fits each gap (1–6). There is one extra paragraph which you do not need to use.

How the microwave oven was invented

The microwave is, these days, a common sight in many kitchens around the world and cherished for the speed at which it heats up food and drink. However, it is a little-known fact that its creation came about almost completely by accident, when a self-taught US engineer named Percy Spencer, who was working on improvements to military hardware, realised a snack he had in his pocket had melted.

1

But Spencer's experience and intelligence led him to the realisation that there were domestic applications for this discovery. He had grown up in a poor family in the backwoods of Maine, in the eastern United States and had minimal formal education. He had also had little or no direct exposure to emerging technologies of the time, such as cars and electrical power.

2

On joining the Navy at the age of 18, he gained a fascination for the radio and taught himself everything he could about the new technology, amongst other things. This was to stand Spencer in good stead after leaving the Navy. He gained employment at the American Appliance Company, which was later renamed the Raytheon Manufacturing Company. He rapidly gained renown as one of their most accomplished engineers.

3

As he did so, he happened to put his hands into his pockets, where he habitually kept his snack. That day, it happened to be a candy bar made from peanuts and caramel. To his surprise, he found that it had turned into a warm, melted mess in his pocket whilst he had

been at work. Had it been a chocolate bar, this would not have been so remarkable, as chocolate becomes liquid at a relatively low temperature. Melting a peanut and caramel bar, however, requires substantially larger amounts of energy.

4

Recognising that it was microwaves produced by the magnetron that had heated it to such a degree, his employer immediately patented the invention. The launch of the first commercial microwave oven came just two years later. Costing around $5,000 (which equates to well over $50,000 these days), it weighed about 340 kg and was almost two metres tall.

5

Eventually, the company worked hard to bring down the price and to create models of a more convenient size, and sales of the microwave oven mushroomed. According to US government figures, in excess of 90% of American homes had microwaves by 1997. Although not all countries have been so quick in embracing this appliance, it's acceptance is growing day by day and it has rapidly become the quickest method of heating up food and drink across the planet.

6

And all of this progress stems from Spencer's realisation that a melting candy bar in his pocket had far greater significance than a trip to the dry cleaners! In 1999, Percy Spencer was finally given his rightful place alongside great inventors such as Thomas Edison and the Wright Brothers in the National Inventors Hall of Fame.

A But Spencer didn't allow this to hold him back. He possessed an unusual instinctive curiosity that led him into employment at a textile mill in a nearby town. This was followed by work at a nearby paper mill. His role there was to assist with the installation of electricity to the plant, despite having had no formal training in electrical engineering.

B In addition to this increasingly-universal appeal, Spencer's work continues to influence research into further uses for radar, especially those which monitor global weather conditions and trap speeding drivers: police radar guns detect the reflections of microwaves to calculate a driver's speed.

C His natural curiosity immediately led him to wonder how exactly this had happened, so Spencer conducted another experiment, this time with an egg. He placed it close to the magnetron and within seconds, it had exploded, splattering cooked egg everywhere, including on his face. On a subsequent occasion, he repeated the experiment with popping corn and was soon sharing popcorn with his team.

D Radar, which had been used extensively by the armed forces, detects enemy aircraft and allows planes to fly at night. It was during his efforts to develop this technology that the unusual side-effect came to light.

E In the 1940s, however, little information was available about the effect microwaves might have on humans, so Spencer never took into account how safe it might be to work and cook with microwaves. Today, we know that the low doses of microwaves generally do little or no harm.

F Developing a reputation there as someone who had an uncanny ability to come up with straightforward fixes to even the most complex of engineering problems, his employer had given him the task of improving radar technology that they were producing for the military. On one occasion, he decided to run some experiments using magnetrons, a high-powered component found inside radars.

G As a consequence of these impracticalities, coupled with the public's mistrust of such a new technology, sales were, perhaps unsurprisingly, poor. The venture ended up losing the company a lot of money, becoming their greatest business failure to date.

2

Rewrite these sentences by changing the <u>underlined</u> words into nouns.

1. The machine <u>weighed</u> about 340 kg.

   The machine was ....

2. The numbers of microwaves in homes is <u>increasing</u> around the world.

   There is an .... in homes around the world.

3. There is nothing that <u>indicates</u> domestic microwaves pose a risk to health.

   There is no ....

4. Spencer's work is still very <u>relevant</u> today.

   Spencer's work .... today.

5. Companies should <u>invest</u> more in finding new applications for microwave technology.

   There should be .... new applications for microwave technology.

6. The public were very slow to <u>accept</u> Spencer's discovery.

   There was a .... Spencer's discovery.

7. Spencer grew up in a very <u>poor</u> family.

   Spencer grew up ....

☑ **Exam tips**

- Before you begin trying to find the answers, quickly read the whole text so you get a good idea of its structure and how it develops.
- Pay particular attention to the sentences before and after each gap because a lot of the most important information that helps you locate the missing paragraph will be there.

Arts and education

☑ Exam task

1 You are going to read a newspaper article about the arts. Six paragraphs have been removed from the article. Choose from the paragraphs A–G the one which fits each gap (1–6). There is one extra paragraph which you do not need to use.

Replacing arts subjects in schools

Despite a lack of resources, we need a commitment to creativity in schools.

In 2006, 84-year-old American novelist, Kurt Vonnegut, wrote a letter to a class of schoolchildren who had asked him to visit. He was too ill to travel, but offered them instead the following lesson for life: 'Practise any art, music, singing, dancing, acting, drawing, painting, sculpting, poetry, fiction, essays, reportage, not to get money and fame, but to experience becoming, to find out what's inside you, to make your soul grow.'

1 ☐

Middle-class parents have long known this; it's why they get their children signed up for music groups before they can walk. Being 'cultured' opens doors even if you don't pursue a career in the arts. Private schools know this too, and usually offer a rich and varied extracurricular programme of artistic activities. But Vonnegut's advice is not so easy to follow for those who have little opportunity or guidance when it comes to the arts.

2 ☐

Perhaps an even greater worry is that creative writing, art, drama and music, once an integral part of the curriculum, are having their status reduced in favour of more obviously 'commercially useful' subjects. In the UK, for example, there has recently been a huge decline in the number of pupils taking qualifications in arts subjects. In a challenging global economy, the arts are increasingly seen as 'soft subjects'.

3 ☐

This observation was reinforced when my 14-year-old son recently chose subject options for the two subsequent academic years. The fact that his school decided to send an accompanying letter assuring parents that the 'soft subjects' would not be considered inferior to maths and sciences by the top universities was telling in itself.

4 ☐

So, if schools and government are unable or unwilling to stem the tide in favour of more 'commercially useful' subjects at the expense of artistic ones, where do those whose career aims do not neatly fall into the commercially useful category turn? Charitable institutions which provide grants and bursaries for talented young people are springing up in many countries, or finding themselves in greater demand. Students who were unable to develop their skills for want of the most basic provision – the cost of a musical instrument or the train fare to attend a drama school audition – are getting their financial needs met, and are also helped in other ways.

5 ☐

But the obvious problem with charities is that, by definition, they can't be everywhere and such an approach is no substitute for a nationwide educational commitment to the arts that reflects the value of the creative sector to the economy and to personal wellbeing. The performing arts should not become luxuries for well-off children, because talent doesn't go with money.

6 ☐

To achieve this worthy aim, governments should consider not only the inclusion of the expressive arts in all state school curricula, but also investment in teachers who can provide art, drama and music outside the timetable, for the less tangible – but no less valuable – purpose of expanding minds and, yes, growing souls.

A But the structure of the timetable they'd decided on, which allowed students to select only one choice between art, music and drama, and none of those if the child also wanted to study a second language, hardly seemed to support that view.

B It's an oddly short-sighted view, and one which has been the subject of campaigns which spell out clearly the contribution of the creative sector to the economy. Encouraging young people to study creative arts is all well and good, but it's also useful to provide them with these figures, to reassure them that there are jobs at the end of it.

C Schools used to provide these, often backed up by community youth projects. But the latter have had their funding cut, and many state-school teachers find their time and resources stretched so thinly that they are unable to provide the kind of music tuition, theatre or gallery trips and after-school clubs that were previously on offer.

D To bridge this potential inequality, carving out a space for all young people to express themselves creatively is essential. It is crucial to developing imagination, curiosity and empathy. These are qualities which can do much to shape a more progressive society.

E This appears to be happening despite assurances from politicians, who firmly reject the suggestion that the arts are somehow considered less important than subjects such as science and maths. The statistics suggest, however, that whatever ministers or congressmen say, a clear disparity appears to have been created.

F One such organisation now supports more than 1,000 individuals through different projects, and counts several established actors among its patrons. Many of them say they wouldn't have been able to get started in their careers without similar backing.

G There's no question that the opportunity to explore creative expression can broaden people of any age's outlook and allow this to happen. And it comes with some pretty positive side-effects: boosting confidence and encouraging empathy and curiosity about the wider world.

2 Complete each sentence 1–8 using the correct form of *have* or *get* + (something) + the past participle of the verb given in brackets.

1. Students were far more likely to .... five years ago than they are now. (their college fees / pay)

2. She .... even though she didn't have much time before the exam. (her revision / do)

3. I don't have a computer so I .... by someone at the college. (my letter of application / type)

4. He .... when the phone call offering him the part came through. (his hair / cut)

5. The students .... three times in the four years before the new head teacher arrived. (the number of drama classes / reduce)

6. The art teacher .... even though the school didn't have much money. (the exhibition trip / subsidise)

7. The theatre .... recently, meaning that it can stage one extra production per year. (its funding / increase)

8. Even .... for the show cost an awful lot of money. (my costume / clean)

 Get it right!

Look at the sentence below. Then try to correct the mistake.

The ladies go to make their hair nice.

Work and training

1

Complete the sentences in the correct tense to make conditional sentences using the verb in brackets.

1. If I .... more training courses, I'd have a better job by now. (do)

2. I always learn something when I .... on a training course. (go)

3. If I .... so little time, I'd look for another job. (not have)

4. The company has said that if the profits are good this year, it .... all staff a bonus. (give)

5. If this computer worked properly, I .... to do my job much more effectively. (be able to)

6. Unless you really change your attitude at work, you .... your job! (lose)

7. Most people .... highly unlikely to continue working if they won $10 million. (be)

8. If you should happen .... a set of keys, please hand them in at reception. (find)

☑ Exam task

2

You are going to read four reviews of training courses from a training company website. For questions 1–10, choose from the reviews (A–D). The reviews may be chosen more than once.

Which reviewer makes the following statements?

I've already recommended the course to several colleagues.	**1**
Being able to contact the trainer after the course has been extremely useful.	**2**
I thought that the pacing of the course was about right.	**3**
There was a bit too much theory and not enough practical work.	**4**
I would have preferred a face-to-face course.	**5**
I was grateful for having a choice of ways of attending the course.	**6**
Some of the materials didn't seem to be particularly relevant.	**7**
The pre-course tasks weren't especially useful.	**8**
I'm impressed by how knowledgeable the instructor was.	**9**
Booking a place on the course was remarkably easy.	**10**

Training course reviews

A This was the first course I'd attended in a while, so I was a bit apprehensive as to whether I'd be able to keep up. There appeared to be others, though, who weren't as familiar with the topic as I was, which meant we spent more time than was intended on learning about the underlying principles, inevitably at the expense of putting what we'd learnt into effect. As a result, we ended up covering less ground than I'd hoped overall. I chose the 'Attend Online' option. If your company's budgets are not high, as was the case with me, not having to cost in travel and accommodation is a real help. From the perspective of viewing slides and keeping up with demonstrations via the virtual environment, it was pretty much as straightforward as registering for the training had been – everything was right there on the screen in front of me, rather than straining to see a whiteboard.

B I must admit, I wasn't exactly filled with optimism when the course information arrived a couple of weeks beforehand. I'd been on so many courses where you spend so much time looking at the underpinning knowledge that you never actually get to see how it works in reality, and what they'd sent pointed to that being the case again. If I wanted that, I'd do a degree in the subject, not a training course! This feeling continued when I had a go at the exercises they'd asked us to do before the first session. I'm pleased to report, though, that all of the preconceptions I'd had about the course were wide of the mark, and several people at my company have applied for it too, after what I'd said about it. The instructor had a real knack of being able to explain some quite complex concepts in such an uncomplicated way and was really happy to talk to people individually after each session.

C Prior to the first session, I was concerned that there wouldn't be sufficient opportunities for questions if I wasn't physically present in the training room. My intuition proved to be true, so I wouldn't do it this way again. That said, the instructor handled the mix of online and face-to-face clients as best he could, and the content was ideal for my line of work. The course had come recommended by my manager, and I appreciate him doing so, as I could apply pretty much everything we covered to my work, even some of the assignments they asked us to do to in preparation. I've exchanged quite a few emails with our instructor since we finished, to clarify a few of the techniques he mentioned, which is above and beyond the call of duty, but he hasn't complained yet. I only wish fewer people had applied as there were too many for one single trainer to cope with, in my opinion.

D What I've often found on training courses is that the promotional material is incredibly appealing, and it's made really simple to reserve a place and pay, but then what you study has little or nothing to do with what you actually signed up for. I'd advise anyone who's interested to give this course a go, though. The content was fascinating, and our course leader was able to answer all of the questions we threw at her, some of which were extremely complex. If training such as this is rushed, the participants can easily become confused. Conversely, if too much time is spent on the detail, everyone loses interest. This avoided falling into either of these traps. The tasks we did prior to the course commencing were spot on, but I wish I could say the same for some of the handouts we got during the session. A minor point on what was an otherwise excellent course.

☑ Exam facts

- This part can be a continuous text or a group of short texts.
- The text or texts are divided into four to six parts, A–D or A–F.
- There are ten questions for all the texts. You have to match each question to the correct text.

© Cambridge University Press and UCLES 2016

The media

1 Match sentences 1–8 with *get* (+ preposition) with the meaning of *get* in a–h.

1. All of the journalists' computers got a virus so the paper was late being published.

2. A lot of the readers didn't get what she was trying to say in the article.

3. The story about the little boy's medical condition really got to a lot of readers.

4. I'm currently researching a story about getting ahead in business.

5. I've really got in with the editor – I think she likes my attitude and the style of my writing.

6. Tim really gets around, doesn't he? He's just done interviews with six famous musicians.

7. I got her in the end by phone – she'd been away in America for a week.

8. How can I get around telling my boss about the mistake with my expenses?

a to have a strong effect on

b to communicate with

c to be very active, especially socially

d to understand

e to avoid

f to catch or to be negatively affected by

g to become close to

h to be successful

☑ Exam task

2 You are going to read an article about the rise and fall in popularity of newspapers. For questions 1–10, choose from the sections (A–D). The sections may be chosen more than once.

In which section does the author

suggest that media tycoons wield too much power?	1
mention the influence that systems of government have on methods of accessing the news?	2
explain how newspapers have adapted in order to survive?	3
describe how individuals' lifestyles have altered the way they consume news media?	4
say that the success of newspapers benefitted another industry?	5
say that ease of access to news changes the level of trust people have in its accuracy?	6
claim that many people would have found living without a newspaper difficult?	7
explain why readers may not want to have access to longer news articles?	8
suggest that the transformation of the newspaper industry is not necessarily a bad thing?	9
suggest that the internet was not responsible for the initial decline in newspaper sales?	10

The rise and fall of the newspaper

A Until relatively recently, newspapers were our primary source of daily news. They must now compete, however, with online news, social media and television in a progressively digital age. The internet is changing the way people get their news, leaving a dwindling audience willing to pay for their daily paper. But given that the form first emerged in early-17th century Europe, it's probably about time the medium got overhauled. Newspapers have witnessed an extraordinary era of change: from the evolution of democratic institutions and political parties to the reshaping of whole countries and continents. The first daily newspaper, *The Courant*, credited the reader with enough intelligence to make up their own minds, printing factual details rather than spinning stories according to any particular opinion. Perhaps current sources could learn something from this approach. However, media magnates soon discovered that if these reports appeared alongside more sensationalist pieces focussing on scandal and gossip, they would attract more interest. A greater readership led to higher revenues from advertising, an industry that grew rapidly alongside the newspaper.

B By the end of the 19th century, newspapers were using a visual template not unlike those of today, and had become the source of not only large profits but also unaccountable political and social influence for their owners – a trend that has continued to the present day. Newspapers prospered in this form for more than 150 years, and in many countries, daily life would have been inconceivable without access to one. But in many places, the continuing existence of newspapers is under threat. The internet has undoubtedly had a profound impact on the industry. The number of sources of available news has mushroomed, which potentially thins out the readership of any one title. Advertisers who once relied on newspapers to reach consumers now prefer to invest on the internet. While printed newspapers increasingly struggle to get by financially, many have turned to the primary cause of their decline in order to attract new revenue: by launching online versions. By doing so, perhaps even newspapers that have been around for hundreds of years will get through this tough time.

C Circulation figures for all types of newspapers, local, regional and national, bear out the fact that, in many Western nations at least, sales of printed newspapers had been falling for many years prior to the emergence of the internet. What is also beyond question, though, is that the arrival and exponential growth of the World Wide Web, leading to near-universal coverage, has accelerated this process greatly. Observing the rapidity and extent of this process around the world provides a fascinating insight into social change. In countries where it's more expedient for people to access news via the internet, this increased convenience seems to also encourage the perception that these online sources are somehow more reliable than printed media. In other parts of the world, however, where there are technological constraints on accessing online sources, or reporting of news is restricted, usually for political reasons, hard-copy newspaper readership is increasing and the printed news industry is flourishing. Globally, therefore, newspapers have clearly not yet been consigned to history.

D Yet we live in an age where speed and convenience have gained precedence over reliability and quality in most aspects of our existence. Regarding the former, newspapers only allow readers to get updated about events some considerable time after they have actually happened, while online users can access them more or less at the moment at which they occur. Printed newspapers, therefore provide a less efficient source of news and, furthermore, do so in a less environmentally-friendly way than the internet, and at a direct cost to the consumer. Moreover, with news also available on tap through social media, consumers are continually bombarded from all sides, and therefore may not wish to have each story explained in great detail, as is the case in much of the printed media. Social media sites have also proven to be one of the most effective means of getting information out rapidly, and on a huge scale: news can now be tweeted before the mainstream media have even started their coverage.

☑ **Exam tips**

- Study the questions carefully first, underlining any key words or phrases.
- Read each section carefully after you have read the questions and try to find the sections of text that each question relates to. Remember that different words will be used in text and question.

Travel and tourism

 Exam task

1 You are going to read an article about the pros and cons of ecotourism. For questions 1–10, choose from the sections (A–D). The sections may be chosen more than once.

In which section does the writer

explain how some non-green businesses exploit the market for ecological holidays? | **1** | |

mention the nature of the relationship between travel firms and local people? | **2** | |

suggest that ecotourism is largely insignificant in solving the world's environmental problems? | **3** | |

exemplify an effect of ecotourism on local wildlife? | **4** | |

describe a negative result of putting the preservation of nature above economic well-being? | **5** | |

explain why conventional tourism benefits a region less than it should? | **6** | |

states the proportion of tourism as a whole that ecotourism represents? | **7** | |

mention how the meaning of important cultural objects can change? | **8** | |

explain the underlying principle on which the ecotourism industry is based? | **9** | |

describe how the financial incentives of ecotourism encourage local people to protect nature? | **10** | |

The pros and cons of ecotourism

A Ecotourism lacks a universally-accepted definition, but is generally regarded as responsible and sustainable travel to natural areas that both conserves the environment and improves the well-being of those living there. At the heart of it is the assumption that in a predominantly capitalist world where nature plays second fiddle to creating wealth, any conservation needs to pay for itself. Money generated from ecotourism is invested back into the conservation of the environment it impacts upon. Supporters argue that, by involving residents in accommodating tourists and acting as guides, for example, ecotourism aids development, both regionally and nationally. In many cases, communities work as equal partners with ecotourism organisations rather than just as employees. However, some detractors point out that the environment is effectively prioritised above the needs of residents. Ecotourism's apparent obsession with this, far from giving a boost to the development of wealth in a community, can actually damage the ability of the majority of inhabitants to lift themselves out of poverty.

B The travel industry contributes over seven trillion dollars to the world economy each year. Having a holiday is big business! Despite what its critics may say, giving a hand to nature in this way has the potential to offer communities some serious economic opportunities as it now accounts for about a fifth of this total, and is continuing to expand. It generates money from natural environments by encouraging tourists to pay for items like accommodation, souvenirs and entrance fees during their stay. Seeing the environment as a valuable resource that communities can use to generate income encourages them to make choices that will help them to take care of it. Yet, inevitably, a fine balance has to be kept to prevent the influx of eco-tourists from degrading the very environment they came to see. Unleashing hundreds of visitors on a delicate ecosystem can, even with the best of intentions, lead to unforeseen environmental impact, such as inadvertently encouraging the animals that live there to become dependent on being fed by tourists.

C It's estimated that, of all the money that travellers spend on traditional holidays, only around half of it stays in the area or country that they visit. The remainder leaks out of the host region and through the books of international hotel chains and tour operators. One intention of ecotourism is to limit as much of this bleeding away of capital from the local economy as possible through maximising the involvement of local businesses and people. The recent wave of successful environmentally-friendly commerce has also led some regular chains and operators to label themselves as ecotourism-friendly by making very minor changes to their existing practices through a process known as greenwashing. They can market themselves in the same way as a genuinely sustainable project by simply changing their cleaning products or recycling more of their waste. Anyone seeking their dream eco-holiday should check the credentials of seemingly environmentally-friendly organisations very carefully indeed. That said, sustainability is becoming much more mainstream and increasing numbers of businesses are genuinely adopting good environmental and social practices.

D One powerful motivation that drives eco-tourism is the chance for holidaymakers to take a look at and experience civilisations that are very different to their own, which in turn can have a positive and affirming knock-on effect on that society. Allowing local people to show their way of life to the world not only tends to make them more positive about tourism, but also empowers them as a community. However, there can of course be less welcome results, such as traditional symbols and artefacts being transformed merely into merchandise to sell to visitors. There can also be disharmony created between previously friendly local factions if one is seen or thought to benefit more than others. Another question ecotourism raises is whether it has a role to play in conservation on anything other than a small scale. By its very nature, it can only take place in a highly limited range of ecosystems as issues of access, susceptibility to damage and the elusive nature of wildlife make some areas inappropriate for exploitation by ecotourism.

2 **Complete the sentences with the correct form of *do, make, have, give* or *take*.**

1. The travel company .... an appeal to its customers to take any rubbish they had back the hotel and use the bins there.

2. We strongly advise all climbers not .... any unnecessary risks when ascending or descending the mountain.

3. Our guide .... a loud laugh when he saw what we were all wearing.

4. Visitors should .... respect for the residents of the village and should not photograph people or their homes without permission.

5. At the beginning of the holiday, we were required .... a promise that we would not touch or harm any of the local plants or animals.

6. We all had jobs when we were on the trek, so after dinner I was often asked if I .... the washing up yet!

7. We really .... a chance by trying such a different holiday this year, but I'm so glad we did.

8. I was so glad that the guide .... us the advice about what to do if we saw a shark because we encountered one on the first dive.

 Get it right!

Look at the sentence below. Then try to correct the mistake.

If we think the club is boring, we should make something about it.

Health and sport

1 Complete the sentences with the correct form of the verbs from the box. Use each word only once.

beat	earn	gain	hurt	injure	reach	win	wound

1. The police officer .... in the shooting has been released from hospital.

2. Our team was .... by two goals in the semi-finals of the tournament.

3. The new star will .... far more money than any of the other players on the team.

4. Thankfully, the supporters were a little shaken, but nobody got .... in the crash.

5. Fundraisers are halfway to .... the figure they need to save the club.

6. The friendly games allow the younger players to .... the experience they need.

7. He .... his wrist a year ago, but it's still sore and stiff some days.

8. We need to .... back fans who've stopped buying season tickets.

2 Correct the common mistakes in the linking words in bold in the text.

In today's society, with the wealth of health information and knowledge at their fingertips, individuals really have no excuse for not making healthy lifestyle choices. For instance, they can ensure that their diet includes all the necessary nutrients, **(1)** .... **althought** not everyone heeds medical guidelines.

(2) .... **Never the less**, not everyone in the world has access to the full range of foods which doctors recommend should appear on our dining table. The sad truth is that every day, millions of people on earth go to bed on an empty stomach. For this second group, choosing to eat well is not an option. **(3)** .... **Either** does this sector of our world population have full access to health care, and they usually lack the supply of medicines that is available in the western world.

Medical intervention is not always the answer. **(4)** .... **Dispite** the fact that advances in medicine mean that there are drug treatments for a large number of illnesses, these health problems have still not disappeared from our planet. **(5)** .... **Eventhough** drugs or vaccines might be administered, they do not always work, **(6)** .... **like**, in certain cases, bugs have evolved to become immune or resistant to the drugs prescribed. As a consequence, medical scientists are faced with the challenge of developing new cures for old illnesses.

In the final analysis, it is said that prevention is better **(7)** .... **then** cure. If we feed our body with a variety of healthy foods, it will receive everything it needs to do its job properly, and hopefully, we will not need to resort to dosing ourselves with pills.

3 The essay in exercise 2 answered the question below. Read the essay again and the notes in the box, then complete the table.

Your class has attended a panel discussion about how people can look after their health.

> **How we can look after our health?**
> - eating well
> - taking medicine
> - keeping fit

Which **two** points did the writer write about?	1	2 ....
Which words and expressions in the essay talk about each point?	3	4 ....
Which point did the writer feel has the greatest impact on people's health?	5	

☑ **Exam task**

4 Your class has listened to a radio programme discussing the ways that sport can benefit people. You have made the notes below:

> **How can sport benefit people?**
> - building community spirit
> - providing role models
> - releasing emotions

> **Some opinions expressed in the discussion:**
> "Being able to cooperate in a team is essential in life."
> "Not all sports stars are good examples to follow."
> "Wanting to win can cause people to behave badly."

Write an essay discussing two of the ways that sport can benefit people. You should explain which way you think is the most effective, giving reasons to support your opinion. Write your answer in 220–260 words.

You may, if you wish, make use of the opinions expressed in the discussion, but you should use your own words as far as possible.

☑ **Exam facts**

- In this part, you write an essay based on two points.
- You have to identify what you think the more important point is, and give your opinion on it explaining your reasons.

Education, learning and work

1a Use the words in the box to complete the expressions for giving opinions.

> as   case   deny   fact   knowledge   opinion   seems   view

1. It seems to be the .... that ....

2. In my ...., ...

3. It .... to me that ....

4. It is common .... that ....

5. The .... is that ....

6. .... I see it, ...

7. Few people would .... that ....

8. In my ...., ...

1b Complete the sentences 1–8 in exercise 1a expressing an opinion or giving a fact about education and learning.

2 Read part of a Part 1 essay question and the notes in the box, then complete the sentences with points you could include in the answer.

Your class has watched a studio discussion on what things a person should consider when choosing a career.

> **What should you consider when choosing a career?**
> - qualifications
> - pay
> - job satisfaction

1. Whenever you decide to learn something new, ...

....

2. Getting into university can be tough, yet ....

....

3. Whichever subject you study, ...

....

4. However much you hate exams, ...

....

5. Stress is bad for us, yet ....

....

6. No matter how much money you may make, ...

....

7. Whatever happens at work, ...

....

8. Wherever you end up working, ...

....

 Exam task

3

Your class has watched a documentary about how workplaces can be made more people-friendly. You have made the notes below:

> **How can workplaces be made more people-friendly?**
> - light and ventilation
> - exercise and breaks
> - decoration

> Some opinions expressed in the discussion:
> "I find it difficult to see my computer screen."
> "Our office is so much better with these plants."
> "There's nowhere to have a coffee except at our desks."

Write an essay discussing two of the ways that workplaces can be made more people-friendly. You should explain which way you think is more effective, giving reasons to support your opinion. Write your answer in 220–260 words.

You may, if you wish, make use of the opinions expressed in the discussion, but you should use your own words as far as possible.

 Exam tips

- Underline the **two** points you are going to write about.
- Write a brief plan of the ideas you want to include.
- When you write your answer, make sure you include both underlined points, and give reasons for your opinions.

Community

1 Rewrite the sentences below using adverbs from the box. Use each adverb once.

apparently	coincidentally	consequently	fortunately
incredibly	regrettably	thankfully	understandably

1. According to my neighbour, some thieves broke into the village shop last night.

....

2. The police were doing their rounds when the break-in took place.

....

3. They were able to stop the robbers from stealing anything from the store.

....

4. It was a shame that a police officer was slightly injured when making the arrest.

....

5. Her injuries are not thought to be serious.

....

6. As a result, she is expected to be released from hospital later today.

....

7. I'm surprised that the shop owners, who were sleeping upstairs, did not hear anything.

....

8. As to be expected, the incident has unsettled local residents, many of whom have been victims of petty crime themselves in the past.

....

2 Match each of the verbs in brackets in sentences 1–8 to the verb or phrase that has a similar meaning (a–h). Put the letters in the boxes. Then complete the sentences with the expressions in the correct form.

a divide	**b** join/come together	**c** allow/approve	**d** work together
e annoy/anger	**f** take part in	**g** decline/become worse	**h** make something possible

1. If you would like to (participate) .... in the event, you have to fill in this form. ☐

2. Everyone in the area (cooperated) .... in the clean-up operation after the floods. ☐

3. Our town has (deteriorated) .... considerably in the last decade. Lots of buildings are in need of repair. ☐

4. The community is (split) .... over how much money should be allocated to the town festival. ☐

5. The neighbours (are united) .... in their concern about the new factory being built near the neighbourhood. ☐

6. The alterations will (facilitate) .... it .... to access the building in a wheelchair. ☐

7. The committee (authorised) .... the plan for an extension. ☐

8. Noisy neighbours can do more than just (irritate) .... you at night. ☐

3 You have been asked to write an essay about making your town more people-friendly. Complete the mind map with ideas for and against suggestions with points from the box. Add two of your own ideas.

> encourage exercise   encourage outdoor play   increased social contact   less pollution
> meeting places   positive for health   reduces fear of falling

 Exam task

4 Your class has listened to a panel discussion about what to do with public buildings which are no longer used. You have made the notes below:

> **What can be done with public buildings which are no longer used?**
>
> - demolish
> - convert into flats
> - community centre
>
> Some opinions expressed in the discussion:
> "There aren't enough places for people to live round here."
> "Renovating old buildings is expensive."
> "There's nowhere for young people to go when the weather's bad."

Write an essay discussing two of the things that can be done with disused buildings in your notes. You should explain which way you think is more effective, giving reasons to support your opinion. Write your answer in 220–260 words.

You may, if you wish, make use of the opinions expressed in the discussion, but you should use your own words as far as possible.

Get it right!

Look at the sentence below. Then try to correct the mistake.

In some places it's happening more quickly and in some places more slowlier.

Arts and entertainment

1a Decide if the adjectives below are positive or negative and write them in the correct column.

absorbing	contrived	disjointed	electric
emotionally charged	family-friendly		original
implausible	mediocre	obvious	overrated
refreshing	riveting	stereotypical	superficial
talented	tasteless	thought-provoking	
touching	unconvincing	wooden	

Positive	Negative

1b Which of the words above could you use to talk about

an actor's performance? ....

....

the development of the story or plot? ....

....

the concept or approach? ....

....

2a Choose the correct alternative to complete the article.

Kevin Walters is, undoubtedly, one of the most skilful storytellers of our times. What makes his novels so remarkable is the clever interweaving of multiple stories, **(1)** *in addition to / what's more* his witty comments and sharp insights into the characters' actions and decisions. In his latest offering, *Storm Brewing*, Walters picks up where his last novel finished: with the birth of Marigold, the newcomer to the Reynold clan. **(2)** *Moreover / Besides* Marigold, there is another new arrival: a mysterious long-lost cousin who no one even knew existed. Although the novel starts off well and we are intrigued by this stranger, the initial buzz quickly wears off. **(3)** *Not once / Not only* do the new characters not add anything special to the story, **(4)** *but / than* they are also devoted far too much importance. **(5)** *Moreover / Over*, too many trivial anecdotes distract the reader's attention away from the main story thread. **(6)** *Evermore / Furthermore,* the hero (mine and everyone's favourite) is killed off half way through and that condemns the whole thing to failure. This is such a pity as his previous novels in the series had had me glued to the page. *Storm Brewing* is not a book that I'll be including in my list to re-read. **(7)** *Whatever / What's more* I won't even be looking to keep my copy. I'm donating it to the local second-hand bookshop **(8)** *along with / moreover* some other rejected tomes.

2b Read the review of the book again. What does the writer like? What does the writer not like?

Likes: ....

Dislikes: ....

 Exam task

3 Read the task. Write your answer in 220–260 words in an appropriate style.

You see the following announcement on a website, 'Fantastic films'.

> **Reader comments wanted**
>
> An entertainment website is putting together a collection of 'greatest' film moments and has asked readers to comment on the website's suggestions for clips. You decide to write a review comparing two of the clips: one that you think should form part of the collection and another that you think shouldn't. Your review should briefly describe each of the clips and should explain why you would recommend one and not the other.

Write your **review**.

 Exam fact

- In this part, you choose one of three tasks. Each task gives the context and purpose for writing and a target reader.

Science

1   **Read the following report and answer the questions below.**

To: The College Principal

Re: The College Science Exhibition

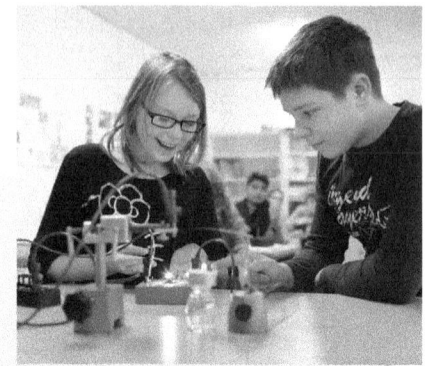

Introduction
The purpose of this report is to consider the attendance and interaction with the exhibits at our first College Science Exhibition and to make some recommendations for the future.

Findings
First and foremost, given the fact that this was the first science exhibition held by the College, it is fair to say that the event exceeded all expectations in terms of visitor numbers.

The visitors
Over the course of five days, more than three hundred visitors passed through the doors. For the most part, these were adults who are relatives of the College students. However, there were also some small children present. Unfortunately, there was a shortage of hands-on activities for this age group, so they soon became bored and restless.

The stands and exhibits
As previously mentioned, the exhibition had not been adequately prepared to cater for small children. Unfortunately, the workshop in the college laboratory was not appropriate for them, so the only attraction they could participate in was the mini hot air balloon experiment. Nevertheless, it was obvious that everyone, including older children, had a passion for science.

Recommendations for improvements
So as to attract a wider audience, I would suggest that the best course of action would be to publicise the event in the local press and on relevant websites. With a view to catering for all, I recommend that there should be more interactive exhibitions and experiments in order to ensure that there is something suited to everyone. If we address these two areas, I am sure that future science exhibitions will build on the success of this first edition.

What was good about the exhibition? ....

What could be improved? ....

2   **Read the question the above report answered, then answer the questions on the next page.**

You are on the student committee at the College where you study. The College recently held a science exhibition. The College Principal has asked you to write a report on the exhibition, explaining its strengths and weaknesses. You should also make recommendations for improvements for future exhibitions.

Did the report opposite:

1. make it clear who the report was for?
2. use headings and clear layout?
3. use a consistent and appropriate register and tone?

4. use a range of language?
5. explain the exhibition strengths and weaknesses?
6. make recommendations for improvements?

3a Some of the words and phrases in the box below are in the report. Find them in the report and underline them.

| in order | in order not to | so | so as to | so as not to | so that | with a view to |

3b Complete the questions using the words or phrases in the box in exercise 3a. Use each word or phrase once.

1. Would you be prepared to pay more .... eat organic food?
2. Do you think robots should do unpleasant jobs .... humans don't have to?
3. Do you agree that the use of cars should be restricted .... worsen pollution and global warming?
4. In your opinion, should people be obliged to keep their mobiles for a stipulated length of time .... we don't have so many discarded phones?
5. Would you say that .... to discover more about Earth, we need to explore other planets?
6. .... encouraging children to like science, what should be done?
7. What steps should science students take .... have an accident in the laboratory?

☑ Exam task

4 Read the task. Write your answer in 220–260 words in an appropriate style.

You have just visited a science museum in the city where you are studying. The school principal has asked you to write a report on the museum, describing what there is to see and do there and explaining why it might or might not be a good place to organise group visits for students at the school.

Write your **report**.

☑ Exam tips

- Take a moment to think about the key features of the task type you have chosen to write about, including the way they should be organised, layout, register, language used, etc.
- Underline the key points in the question and make sure you cover all the parts of the question in your answer.

Work

1   **Match 1–10 to a–j to form expressions used at the end of letters.**

1.	Yours	**a**	soon.
2.	Best	**b**	sincerely,
3.	Looking forward to	**c**	regards,
4.	Yours	**d**	wishes,
5.	I hope	**e**	faithfully,
6.	Keep	**f**	best,
7.	Kind	**g**	hearing from you.
8.	I look forward	**h**	to your reply.
9.	All the	**i**	in touch!
10.	Write	**j**	to hear from you soon.

Which of the endings are more <u>formal</u>, <u>semi-formal</u> or <u>informal</u>?

2   **Read the two exam questions asking you to write a letter giving advice and answer the questions.**

1. Which one asks for the more formal letter?
2. Which of the questions asks you to do more than just give advice on things to do?
3. What language could you use to provide this other information?

Question 1

You work for an international company. A colleague from the New Zealand office of your company is coming to work in your office for four months. Write a letter to this colleague, giving details of your branch and the people who work there. You should also give some advice about the things he/she could do in their free time while he/she is in your country.

Question 2

You have received a letter from an English-speaking friend:

> My new job is great, and next month, my company is sending me to do a three-week language course – guess where – in your town!
>
> I'll be free four evenings and one weekend, so I'd like your advice please on where to go, what to do and the best way to practise my language while I'm there.
>
> Thanks,
>
> Rodrigo

Write a **letter** to your friend giving your opinion and advice.

3 Read the questions again and complete the table to say what language you would use for each question.

		Question 1, 2 or both?
greetings	**a** *Dear Rodrigo,*	
	b *Dear Ms Baker,*	
starting the letter	**a** *I am writing to give you information and my advice . . .*	
	b *Thanks for your letter. Great news that . . .*	
contractions	**a** yes (*I'm, You'd, You'll . . .*)	
	b no (*I am, You would, You will . . .*)	
language for making suggestions	**a** *What about . . . ? Try . . . Take it from me . . . I'd say that . . . You can take your pick . . .*	
	b *I would highly recommend . . . You could try . . . Might I suggest . . . Another alternative might be . . .*	
phrases to talk about suitability	**a** *would be ideal for you might (not) appeal would suit you best*	
	b *your sort of thing You might fancy might tempt you*	

☑ Exam task

4 Read the task. Write your answer in 220–260 words in an appropriate style.

You are a university student and you see an advert for teaching assistants with good sports or craft skills at an international summer camp. You decide to apply for one of the roles and write to the Human Resources Manager at the company, explaining what your skills are and why you would be suitable, what kind of work you would like to do and why the company should consider your application.

Write your **letter.**

◎ Get it right!

Look at the sentence below. Then try and correct the mistake.

Me and my cousins used to collect all sorts of things.

Travel

1 Complete the sentences with the expressions from the box.

| at your leisure   low-cost   low season |
| off-the-beaten-track   on a shoestring   once-in-a-lifetime |
| overrun with tourists   uninterrupted views |

1. At peak times, city hotspots which are totally .... are facing angry backlashes from residents who are tired of the crowds.

2. Travelling .... is not for everyone, particularly those who find it hard to give up certain luxuries.

3. Later, you will have several hours to explore the area .... Your guide will not be accompanying you.

4. The best time to visit popular destinations is during the ...., when the tourist hordes are staying home.

5. The lakeside retreat offers .... across the valley.

6. Thanks to .... airlines, people who had previously never been able to afford to fly are now doing so.

7. The resort's .... location ensures complete tranquillity. No major roads or airports are in sight.

8. A 12-year-old local dancer who has won a .... trip to the Big Apple described it as 'a dream come true'.

2 Complete sentences with the words and phrases from the boxes.

| as a result | for that reason | in view of the fact that | that is why |

1. .... we have an early morning departure, we should all retire to bed.

2. On our arrival at the hotel, our rooms were not ready. .... we left our luggage with the concierge and went to explore the town.

3. .... of not sticking to the speed limit, too many motorists are risking their own lives as well as those of other road users.

4. There had been an accident. .... there was a tailback of traffic for approximately a kilometre.

| consequently | since | therefore | thanks to |

5. The airport was closed due to fog. ...., there were huge delays to flights.

6. .... the locals are well-known for their hospitality, newcomers are being attracted to this corner of the world.

7. .... the amenities it offers, this hotel ticks all the boxes.

8. Backpacking round different parts of the world is still relatively cheap. ...., many students do this in their gap year.

 Exam task

3

Read the task. Write your answer in 220–260 words in an appropriate style.

You study at an international college in your country. Your history teacher is planning a one-day study trip for your class and has asked the students for suggestions. Write a proposal considering two or three different places for history students to visit in the area and recommend which one of these places would be preferable for a one-day study visit.

Write your **proposal.**

4

After you have written your answer, check that you have done the following things:

A proposal

1. A proposal should be clearly organised, using headings.

   Did you use headings?

   Are the different sections in a logical order?

2. Candidates are expected to make suggestions and evaluations.

   Did you suggest a destination, and the best way to get there?

   Did you put forward some suggestions for activities to do?

   Did you say why these ideas were good ones?

3. The recommended course of action should be clear to the reader, who could be a supervisor or a classmate.

   Did you write to the right person?

   Do you think she/he could use the information in your proposal to make a decision?

Arts and Literature

☑ Exam task

1 ◀» Track 1 **You will hear three different extracts. For questions 1–6, choose the answer (A, B or C) which fits best according to what you hear. There are two questions for each extract.**

Extract One

You hear two friends discussing the topic of reading books in printed or electronic form.

1. The woman admits that when she reads printed novels

   A she misses out the more boring parts.

   B she looks ahead to see what will happen.

   C she fails to take care of the book.

2. Which aspect of their enjoyment of reading do the friends agree about?

   A how much it depends on the quality of writing

   B how convenient electronic books are

   C how pleasant it is to own a printed book

Extract Two

You hear a woman telling a friend about a book he gave her.

3. What is she doing in the conversation?

   A describing the book's plot

   B describing the main characters' behaviour

   C describing her own reaction to the book

4. Why does she mention the book's cover?

   A to suggest that it failed to reflect its contents

   B to criticise a weakness in the book's plot

   C to explain why the book has sold well

Extract Three

You hear two writers talking about their daily routine.

5. When talking about finding ideas for writing, the man says that

   A he uses emails as a source of stimulation for stories.

   B he looks for original plots in newspaper stories.

   C he avoids depending on the internet for storylines.

6. They both think that taking exercise

   A is a pleasant way of taking a break from writing.

   B is effective for helping to think clearly.

   C is necessary but unappealing.

☑ Exam facts

- In this part you hear three unrelated texts.
- Each one involves two speakers.
- They are taken from a wide range of contexts.

© Cambridge University Press and UCLES 2016

2 Choose the correct verb in each sentence.

1. Greg Parson's book *Charity At Home* was *declared / designated* winner of the National Literature Prize.

2. I really do *indicate / urge* you to read *War and Peace* – it's one of the greatest novels ever written.

3. Julie *reassured / confided* in me that she was thinking of giving up her creative writing course.

4. 'I hate having to write so many essays,' *grumbled / presumed* Freddy.

5. Journalist Pete Withers is refusing to *dispute / disclose* his sources to the police.

6. Helen *reasoned / vowed* that the murderer in the whodunnit couldn't be the cook as he had no real motive.

7. The newspapers are *mentioning / speculating* that the book prize will be won by a relative newcomer.

8. The law *stipulates / notifies* that a journal cannot publish false information about a living person.

3 Complete the second sentence so that it is similar in meaning to the first sentence.

1. 'I'll send you a copy of my poem to read,' Noah said to Dee.
   Noah promised .... a copy of the poem he'd written.

2. 'I don't think Archer's latest thriller will sell as well as his last one,' said Sophie.
   Sophie predicted that Archer's latest thriller .... as well as his previous one.

3. According to this article, they're making the book *Destination X* into a film.
   This article says that the book *Destination X* .... into a film.

4. 'I'm finding writing my new novel rather boring,' said Sam.
   Sam complained that .... his new novel rather boring.

5. 'Why don't you join our reading group?' Maria said to Anna.
   Maria suggested to .... should join the reading group.

6. 'My daughter has had a novel published,' said Mrs Day.
   Mrs Day boasted that .... a novel published.

7. 'Don't forget to take that book back to the library,' Harry said to Ben.
   Harry .... the book back to the library.

8. Everybody thought the book was far better than the film.
   The book was said .... far better than the film.

9. 'I honestly didn't touch the painting!' Martha said.
   Martha completely .... the painting.

10. 'I have the same opinion as you about *Hamlet*, Ruth. It's Shakespeare's greatest play,' said Matt.
    Matt .... that *Hamlet* was Shakespeare's greatest play.

Human behaviour

☑ **Exam task**

1 🔊 **Track 2** You will hear three different extracts. For questions 1–6, choose the answer (A, B or C) which fits best according to what you hear. There are two questions for each extract.

Extract One

You hear two friends talking about travelling on public transport.

1. They both say that commuters

   A generally avoid interacting with others.

   B are usually willing to help passengers with difficulties.

   C tend to feel more relaxed when there are fewer people.

2. What point is the woman making about the seating?

   A It can often become uncomfortable over longer periods.

   B It can be designed to help people feel more secure with others.

   C It can be hard for people to get the seat they prefer to sit in.

Extract Two

You hear two friends discussing the use of social media.

3. What does the woman think is a strength of hers?

   A She responds calmly to criticism.

   B She expresses her views fearlessly.

   C She assesses other people's comments accurately.

4. What aspect of social media does the man disapprove of?

   A people giving an overly positive impression of their lives

   B people paying too much attention to unreliable news

   C people trying to draw attention to themselves

Extract Three

You hear part of a radio programme in which two journalists are discussing surveys.

5. What does the man say about some surveys of human behaviour?

   A The sample size they use is usually too small to be accurate.

   B The influence they have on how people make choices is excessive.

   C The results rely too heavily on what people say.

6. Why does the woman give the example of a soft drinks manufacturer?

   A to illustrate the difficulties of doing research using surveys

   B to support an alternative approach to research based on surveys

   C to criticise the methods of research used in a particular survey

2 Choose an appropriate adverb meaning the same as the words in brackets in each sentence.

reluctantly	nostalgically	helplessly	aggressively	willingly
	fearlessly	affectionately		

1. People whose parents treated them .... (in a loving way) tend to have similar parenting styles with their own children.

2. I was pleased to see a young man give up his seat .... (without reluctance) to an elderly man on the bus.

3. Unfortunately, people are more likely to behave .... (in a hostile way) towards outsiders than members of their own group.

4. .... (Showing little desire to do it) the young child handed over the money he'd just found in the street to his mother.

5. Sally stood up .... (showing no signs of being frightened) at the meeting and said she disagreed with the director.

6. The children were all giggling .... (without self-control) for most of the film.

7. The old man spoke .... (in a way that showed sadness at the passing of time) about his childhood growing up in Kenya.

3 These sentences all contain reported speech. Decide whether the structures in each sentence are correct (*C*) or not (*N*). Correct the incorrect sentences.

1. The 1989 study said that most respondents believe that their driving skills were above average. ....
....

2. Marcus said that he had tried to contact Gemma but that she had ignored his messages. ....
....

3. Our teacher told us that social psychology is the study of human behaviour in social settings. ....
....

4. Richard told me that he's going to try to give up smoking before the course ended. ....
....

5. The psychologist B.F. Skinner said that if you are old, it is easier to change your environment than your behaviour. ....
....

6. Liam said that he's been having stress-related nightmares during the previous month. ....
....

☑ **Exam tips**

- Focus on the stem or question rather than the options when you listen. Choose the option that most closely matches what was said.
- The answers to the questions could come at any stage in the recording, so don't expect to hear things in the same order as in the questions.

Travel

  ✓ Exam task

1 🔊 Track 3 **You will hear three different extracts. For questions 1–6, choose the answer (A, B or C) which fits best according to what you hear. There are two questions for each extract.**

Extract One

You hear two students talking about spending a gap year in Australia before going to university.

1. The girl thinks most British teenagers she met chose Australia because of

    A the variety of things to do and see there.

    B the lack of difficulties presented by the language.

    C the opportunities to visit Southeast Asia on the way.

2. What was the biggest issue the boy faced during his time in Australia?

    A finding affordable accommodation

    B having to do very long bus journeys

    C getting suitable work to cover his costs

Extract Two

You hear two friends discussing the purpose of travelling.

3. What does the man consider important when he travels?

    A seeing as much as possible of a new place

    B avoiding the routes taken by other travellers

    C making friends with people from the country he is in

4. Why does the woman mention getting lost?

    A to suggest that a difficulty can bring benefits

    B to illustrate a risk of travelling in unfamiliar places

    C to explain why people react to situations differently

Extract Three

You hear two colleagues talking about a trip to a conference.

5. When discussing the talks they will give, they both

    A plan to improve the presentation of the material for the talk.

    B hope to get some feedback before giving the talk.

    C feel a need to do some more practice of their talk.

6. What does the woman say about the trip?

    A She is worried about what she needs to pack.

    B She is satisfied with the travel arrangements.

    C She is looking forward to being in a different environment.

2 Choose the correct word, a, b or c, for each space.

1. Claire's main .... for going to Nepal was to see the Himalayas.

   a motivation   **b** order   **c** point

2. In .... to make the most of your visit to Canada, I'd recommend going in summer when you'll be able to travel around more easily.

   a purpose   **b** intention   **c** order

3. If you stay in a cheap hotel in New York, it really defeats the whole .... of flying there business class.

   a order   **b** point   **c** basis

4. Seeing new places and learning about their people and history gives me a real sense of .... in life.

   a grounds   **b** motive   **c** purpose

5. Tomasz always makes a .... of visiting the important museums when he goes to a new city.

   a purpose   **b** point   **c** motive

6. I have no .... of changing my ticket just because you've suddenly decided to go somewhere different.

   a grounds   **b** motivation   **c** intention

3 Complete the sentences with the phrases from the box.

could have been   needn't be booked   will leave   would have enjoyed   would rather take

1. The plane journey from Dallas to Perth .... a lot more tiring than it was.

2. They .... the camping trip more if it hadn't rained the whole time.

3. Your tickets .... any longer than a few days in advance of your journey.

4. We .... a taxi than go to the airport by bus.

5. Kate .... it till the last minute before she books a plane ticket.

⊙ Get it right!

Look at the sentence below. Then try to correct the mistake.

A time in history in which I would liked to have been present is the Victorian era.

Science

1 Complete each sentence with the correct spelling of the missing word. Three letters are given for each word.

1. More investment will be n _ _ _ s _ _ _ y if we're to develop effective sustainable energy sources.

2. The development of penicillin was one of the greatest a _ _ _ _ v _ _ _ _ _ s in the history of medicine.

3. Science subjects at school are often divided into the three areas of biology, physics and c _ _ _ _ s _ _ y.

4. The b _ s _ _ _ _ s community are always interested in the commercial potential of new scientific developments.

5. Don't attempt to do this experiment alone as you will need an a _ _ _ s _ _ _ t.

6. Joanna's a _ _ _ m _ _ _ _ _ _ _ n on the university campus is a short walk from the science blocks.

7. Scientists are always eager to understand more about the b _ _ _ _ n _ _ g of the universe.

8. The standard scientific unit of m _ _ _ _ r _ _ _ _ t is the SI, for example, the metre, the second or the kilogram.

9. Scientific r _ s _ _ _ _ h generally involves planning and conducting experiments and analysing results.

10. A p _ _ c _ _ _ _ _ _ _ t is a medical professional who evaluates and studies behaviour and mental processes.

2 Choose the correct alternative for each sentence.

1. Haven't *some / these* experiments like this been done before? I'm sure I've read about them.

2. Scarcely *some / any* of the students had read the professor's book before his lecture.

3. There are countless sci-fi movies in which *much / few* of the science fails to reflect what is really possible.

4. Unless science is taught in a way that encourages pupils to participate, not *all / every* children will be interested in it.

5. *Both / Either* scientists agreed that there is likely to be more progress in this field next year.

6. Whether time travel is possible or not is an incredibly complex area, and there's *no / a* simple answer to the question.

7. At present we cannot look at a brain and know what it is thinking, though *either / such* things may be possible one day.

8. Science is *a / the* time-consuming process, and it often takes decades for major discoveries to translate into treatments.

9. When carrying out this experiment *those / certain* rules must be obeyed, and I will describe them in detail shortly.

10. The questions in this survey take *little / a little* account of the results of the previous one.

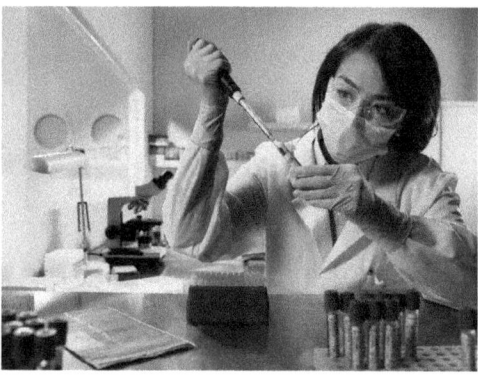

✓ **Exam task**

🔊 Track 4 **You will hear a woman called Camilla Doyle introducing a science fair. For questions 1–8, complete the sentences with a word or short phrase.**

Science fairs

Camilla admits that she has seen rather a lot of **(1)** .... at previous science fairs.

Camilla was amazed that one scientist, David Nelson, tried to construct a mini nuclear fusion reactor in his **(2)** ....

The scientists who created a diesel hybrid racing car are working on redeveloping its **(3)** ....

Camilla claims that there may be many possible uses in industry for Joe Higson's machine that can detect certain **(4)** ....

Camilla thinks there will be developments in new **(5)** .... that helps spacecraft avoid hitting objects in their path.

A group of students produced a **(6)** .... that recorded accurate measurements of weather events.

Many journalists have shown an interest in a special type of underwater vehicle that may be used to study the **(7)** ....

While talking to scientists with exhibits at the science fair, Camilla was most impressed by their **(8)** ....

✓ **Exam facts**

- In this part, you will hear a monologue directed at a non-specialist audience.
- You have to complete eight gaps in the text with words you hear in the recording.

Volunteering

☑ Exam task

1 🔊 Track 5 **You will hear a young man called Sam Parker talking about doing volunteer work in other countries. For questions 1–8, complete the sentences with a word or short phrase.**

International volunteering

Some countries have specific rules about the **(1)** .... of people who volunteer for work there.

Sam learnt most about **(2)** .... during his time at a safari park.

Sam appreciated being taught to use **(3)** .... and basic tools to build a hut.

Sam says that **(4)** .... is the minimum commitment recommended for a placement.

A volunteer should not expect an organisation to fit in with his or her **(5)** ...., according to Sam.

Sam says that it is best to have a clear idea of who the **(6)** .... are of any agency that finds a position for volunteers.

According to Sam, those volunteering projects that are most effective provide **(7)** .... for volunteers to read before going.

Sam was surprised that he never suffered from **(8)** .... during his time volunteering.

☑ Exam tips

- Look at the gaps and using the context of the sentence and words around them try to guess what sort of words might fit there.
- Remember that most gaps will require just one word, though up to three may occasionally be required.
- Do not try and paraphrase the information you hear. Instead, write the exact words that are used in the text.

2a In each group, 1, 2 and 3, match the words that have similar meanings.

1. thoroughly / pretty / sort of / fairly / kind of / totally

   a .... + ... b .... + ... c .... + ...

2. completely / rather / virtually / somewhat / almost / absolutely

   a .... + ... b .... + ... c .... + ...

3. slightly / terribly / mostly / generally / awfully / a bit

   a .... + ... b .... + ... c .... + ...

2b Now complete each sentence with an alternative word from exercise 2a to the one in brackets.

1. Volunteering has become .... (terribly) popular as an activity for young people in their gap year before university.

2. Although farmwork was .... (somewhat) tiring initially, we soon got used to it.

3. 'I'm .... (sort of) nervous about heading off abroad on my own,' Jilly admitted.

4. Joan .... (totally) enjoyed her time working as a volunteer in a safari park in Kenya.

5. There were so many interesting activities on offer that it was .... (virtually) impossible to decide which one to choose.

3 Complete each sentence with the correct form of the word in brackets.

1. Volunteering abroad is an .... rewarding way to see the world and learn about different cultures. (believe)

2. I never suffered from .... during my trip because I met so many other great people. (lonely)

3. Juliette always writes .... about her volunteering experiences on her online blog. (passion)

4. Increased tourism has had huge economic .... for the country. (significant)

5. It's really .... how good doing something worthwhile makes you feel. (notice)

6. If you don't like being ...., why not head off abroad somewhere and do some volunteering? (employ)

7. Although it may be hard work, being a volunteer, you live a more natural kind of .... if you are doing physical work. (exist)

8. Volunteering may be a very .... solution to some of the world's problems, but at least people get the chance to learn how others live. (perfect)

9. During his gap year, Max helped in a free school for .... children. (advantage)

Biography

☑ **Exam task**

1 🔊 **Track 6 You will hear part of a talk by a woman called Ellie Matthews about her life working as a writer and illustrator of children's books. For questions 1–8, complete the sentences with a word or short phrase.**

Life as a children's book author and illustrator

As a child, Ellie felt that adults saw her as having a strong **(1)** ....

After studying at art college Ellie was disappointed to be turned down for a job at a gallery and an **(2)** ....

Ellie's first well-paid piece of work was doing the illustrations for **(3)** ....

The most striking feature of the character Carly in Ellie's first successful book, *Carly*, was her **(4)** ....

Ellie found reading **(5)** .... from the time of her own schooldays helpful for creating the details of Carly's life.

The biggest factor in Ellie's decision to move from Britain to live in the USA was her love of its **(6)** ....

When working on her illustrations, Ellie says she is very fussy about what kind of **(7)** .... she uses.

Ellie feels that having children of her own has given her **(8)** .... that she hopes to pass on to others.

---

2 **Complete each sentence with the correct form of the verbs given in brackets.**

1. Harold .... most weekends of first year of his university degree working part time in a burger bar, but the need to do this .... when he inherited a sum of money from his grandfather. (spend / remove)

2. Vernasso's earliest works were shown at an art gallery in Paris that .... by a German art collector who later .... one of the most important art dealers in Europe. (open / become)

3. At the outbreak of war, they .... in the countryside, and unlike many writers of the time both .... able to continue working throughout the period of the war. (live / be)

4. My husband and I .... until 1973, even though both of us .... at the same university for three years. (meet / study)

5. Larkson's talents as a footballer .... by a coach who contacted a major team to say that he .... a potential star. (spot / find)

3a Match the verbs 1–12 with the words they collocate with in each group.

1. draw	concern
2. cause	a move
3. make	heart
4. take	attention

5. draw	a contribution
6. cause	a conclusion
7. make	exception
8. take	distress

9. draw	embarrassment
10. cause	support
11. make	charge
12. take	a point

3b Complete each sentence with the correct form of a suitable collocation from exercise 3a.

1. My mother always .... of escorting me to my ballet classes, even when I was 14 years old and would have preferred to go alone.

2. Her talents as a tennis player only started .... from adults when she reached the age of 12.

3. I used to go red a lot as a teenager, as my father talking loudly about my achievements frequently .... me ....

4. Although her very first singing auditions were unsuccessful, she .... from the fact that she received a lot of praise for the power of her voice.

Get it right!

Look at the sentences below. Then try to correct the mistake.

It was planned for the next day, a boat trip on the River Thames, but the weather was terrible and we couldn't go.

Work and money

☑ Exam task

1 🔊 **Track 7** You will hear part of an interview with two graphic designers called Anita Dickinson and Joe Connolly in which they talk about going freelance. For questions 1–6, choose the answer (A, B, C or D) which fits best according to what you hear.

1. Anita admits feeling unsure about leaving her job with a big company because
   A she lacked sufficient experience in her field.
   B she was concerned about her financial prospects.
   C she doubted her ability to work for herself.
   D she was anxious about the opinion of her colleagues.

2. What does Joe say about when he first started working freelance?
   A It was more complicated than he'd expected.
   B He resented having less free time than before.
   C It was necessary to have the right attitude to work.
   D He found it easy to find clients through his website.

3. Joe confesses that having to work at home on his own is
   A a relief after working in a busy office.
   B a cause of loneliness for him at times.
   C something that he avoids as much as possible.
   D something that he thought he would dislike.

4. When asked about self-discipline, Anita claims that
   A she checks her daily work output very carefully.
   B she is rarely tempted away from work by social media.
   C she needs certain apps to keep her focussed on work.
   D she is often forced to change her working hours to fulfil contracts.

5. Anita and Joe agree that keeping up to date with trends is
   A less important than being a specialist in one area.
   B difficult when balanced against other demands on time.
   C one of the most enjoyable sides of their work.
   D not as challenging as they'd expected it to be.

6. What does Joe think is the reason for his success as a freelancer?
   A He has effective negotiating skills.
   B He makes sure he has good relations with clients.
   C He gets plenty of personal recommendations.
   D He offers his services at the right price.

☑ Exam facts

- In this part, you listen to longer interviews and discussions and are tested how well you understand the speakers' attitudes and opinions.
- You may also be tested on whether they agree, their feelings, the purpose of the interaction and details.

2 Choose the correct alternative to complete each sentence.

1. Roberta *admitted / claimed* feeling nervous about leaving his job to start his own company.

2. The head of the sales department *proposed / confessed* that she was disappointed with the year's results.

3. I *acknowledge / recommend* investing in a safe fund that will give you a steady level of interest on your money rather than a riskier fund with higher potential earnings.

4. Although Mark *denied / suggested* exaggerating how much money he made when he sold his flat, it was obvious the figure couldn't be as high as he said.

5. Sean's parents *insisted / opposed* that he should study law even though he wanted to study business.

6. My mother *admitted / suggested* that I get a part-time job to earn some extra money during the summer holidays.

7. Many people *oppose / contradict* tax rises, despite wishing to see improved public services.

8. The company spokesperson *claims / recommends* that its products are fantastic value.

3 Look at the position of the adverbs (or adverbial phrases) underlined in each sentence. Decide if the position is correct or incorrect. Match each sentence to one of the reasons below, a–h.

1. A large investment involves <u>inevitably</u> some risk.

2. <u>Clearly</u>, it's impossible to avoid hard work if you want to be successful in life.

3. Nurses in most countries are <u>predominantly</u> female.

4. In its first year, the company made any money <u>barely</u> but things improved later.

5. Joe works <u>a lot of the time</u> from home.

6. The company made heavy spending cuts last year. <u>As a result</u>, over 10% of employees were laid off.

7. Thankfully, discrimination against women at work is decreasing <u>in many countries</u>.

8. Shareholders <u>always</u> are interested in getting a good return on their investment.

a   Correct. A viewpoint adverb usually goes in front position in the sentence.

b   Incorrect. Adverbs of frequency usually go before the main verb but after the verb *be*.

c   Correct. Connecting adverbs usually go in front position.

d   Correct. A focussing adverb often goes in mid-position before the main verb but after the verb *be*.

e   Incorrect. An adverb of degree usually goes in mid-position before the main verb.

f   Correct. Adverbs of place, especially longer ones, usually go in end position, but they can also go in front position. In this case there is another adverb in front position, so it is not suitable.

g   Incorrect. A viewpoint adverb usually goes in front position, but can also go in end position, or midposition before the main verb.

h   Incorrect. Adverbs of place usually go before adverbs of time, and longer adverbs usually go after shorter ones.

Health and sport

☑ Exam task

1

◀)) **Track 8 You will hear an interview in which two people called Claire MacBride and Shaun Kale are talking about training to run in a charity marathon. For questions 1–6, choose the answer (A, B, C or D) which fits best according to what you hear.**

1. When Claire started her marathon training programme, she felt

    A   encouraged by the reaction of others.
    B   amazed at her own self-discipline.
    C   determined to establish new habits.
    D   aware of the size of the task ahead.

2. What mistake does Shaun believe he made in his marathon preparation?

    A   not being sufficiently fit at the start
    B   overtraining in the early days
    C   not realising the importance of motivation
    D   choosing an unsuitable training plan at first

3. Claire says that after she got injured she

    A   considered the prospect of giving up her training.
    B   accepted the necessity of getting plenty of rest.
    C   paid attention to the recommendations of a trainer.
    D   made the decision to modify her training plan.

4. What does Claire suggest about training on winter mornings?

    A   It was helpful to pay attention to the sounds she heard.
    B   It was hard without a running companion.
    C   It was necessary to prepare herself mentally.
    D   It was depressing to be running in the dark.

5. When asked about his running speed on the marathon, Shaun reveals his

    A   lack of faith in technology.
    B   desire to achieve a good race time.
    C   worries about finishing the race.
    D   pride in his increased fitness.

6. For both Claire and Shaun, their experience of the marathon event as a whole was

    A   full of highly emotional moments.
    B   more satisfying than they had been led to believe.
    C   made easier by the support they received from the crowd.
    D   stressful as a result of unexpected issues.

2a Match 1–7 to the most suitable definition a–g.

1. spur on	**a** gradually increase
2. build up	**b** become involved in a difficult situation without intending to
3. wear off	**c** avoid
4. factor in	**d** cncourage
5. refrain from	**e** include (when trying to understand something)
6. turn out	**f** gradually disappear
7. let oneself in for something	**g** go to watch an event

2b Complete the sentences with the correct form of the expressions in exercise 2a to complete the sentences. You may need to change the form of the verb.

1. The noise and excitement of the crowd seemed to .... the players to try even harder during the closing stages of the match.

2. The burning feeling in his shoulder began to return once the effect of the painkillers ....

3. These research results don't make sense unless the age of the patients ....

4. You need to make sure you eat healthily to .... your strength after your illness.

5. Andy decided not to get the annual gym membership because he didn't want to .... something he might regret.

6. Please .... smoking in both indoor and outdoor areas.

7. The number of people who .... to watch the basketball final exceeded all expectations.

3 Complete the sentence with the correct verb forms in brackets to make conditional sentences.

1. If I .... (factor) in the importance of mental training when I prepared for the marathon, I .... (tackle) the race better.

2. I reckon they .... (score) another goal if they .... (have) a couple more minutes of injury time in last night's match.

3. Marta .... (not try) hypnotherapy in her efforts to quit smoking, if you .... (not spend) as long as you did convincing her to give it a go.

4. I kept telling Ben that if he .... (not eat) that burger and chips so fast, he .... (not end) up with indigestion, but he didn't listen.

5. Vasilova .... (have) more chance in the match if she .... (not be) injured for so much of the previous season.

6. There .... (be) many more unnecessary deaths from treatable diseases in the 20th century if it .... (not be) for the discovery of penicillin.

☑ **Exam tips**

- If the audio is an interview, use the interviewer's questions to guide you through the six questions.
- If the audio text is a discussion between two speakers, listen carefully for cues to show that the topic is moving on. This will guide you through the six multiple-choice questions.
- Remember that the correct option may be implied rather than clearly stated.

Brain and senses

  Exam task

1

🔊 **Track 9** You will hear two students called Jolie and Alan talking about a TV series they watch called 'The Sensing Brain'. For questions 1–6, choose the answer (A, B, C or D) which fits best according to what you hear.

1. What point is made about a good sense of smell?
   - **A** It is a natural ability that is hard to improve.
   - **B** Some people have a far better one than others.
   - **C** It can be developed in a similar way to other abilities.
   - **D** Some people exaggerate how poor theirs is.

2. What does Jolie say about describing perfumes?
   - **A** Experts use a vocabulary that is hard for people to understand.
   - **B** Some perfumes are too complex to be described.
   - **C** Ordinary people sometimes fail to use words appropriately.
   - **D** Some perfumes require a particularly specialist vocabulary.

3. What does Alan say about synthetic smells?
   - **A** They are able to mislead people into believing they are natural.
   - **B** They have a greater effect on people than natural ones.
   - **C** They are seen as more unpleasant than natural ones.
   - **D** They vary in their popularity with the public.

4. When talking about smell and the brain, Alan reveals
   - **A** his belief that humans have superior smelling abilities to some animals.

   - **B** his doubts about whether humans and animals should be compared.
   - **C** his suspicion of those who report on experiments in the media.
   - **D** his awareness of the problems of conducting accurate studies.

5. Alan and Jolie agree that listening to music while studying
   - **A** is beneficial if the music chosen is not too emotional.
   - **B** has an undesirable effect on their powers of concentration.
   - **C** helps the mind to focus on things that are important.
   - **D** has different effects depending on the material being studied.

6. When talking about the next episode of the programme, Jolie shows that she
   - **A** is worried about the amount of information there is on the internet.
   - **B** has doubts about how good the internet is for people.
   - **C** believes the internet makes her own life more difficult.
   - **D** trusts in her brain's capacity to evaluate information on the internet.

  Get it right!

Look at the sentence below. Then try to correct it.

You can find out everything you want, if just you press the button.

2 ▶ **Complete the sentences with the correct words from the box.**

| one | ones | either | neither | not | ours | so | such | those |

1. I don't think the internet has a harmful effect on the brain. And it isn't bad for your memory ....

2. 'This new study about the brain is very interesting.' 'Yes, ... I gather.' I've heard it's worth reading.

3. The brains of mice are much smaller than ....

4. It seems everyone can improve their sense of smell. Even .... who have difficulty initially show improvements with practice.

5. I've got a terrible memory. I'd love to have a better ....

6. I adore light flowery perfumes, but I'm less keen on heavy spicy ....

7. A: There's this guy who can memorise a 50 digit number just by looking at it for a few seconds.
   B: I find it hard to believe .... a thing.

8. Harvey doesn't find music helps his concentration while studying, and .... does Becky.

9. A: Do you think your brainpower will improve as you get older?
   B: I expect ...., unless, of course, I do regular brain training!

3 ▶ **Complete the sentences with the words in brackets in the most appropriate order.**

1. Lucy .... in brain surgery.
   (almost / is / specialise / going / certainly / to)

2. There .... further research into this area.
   (than / be / is / likely / to / more)

3. It .... 'designer babies' may become a reality.
   (that / probable / increasingly / looks)

4. The doctors .... the new treatment will work.
   (not / are / that / sure / absolutely)

5. The study shows that some people .... from memory problems than others.
   (more / far / likely / suffer / are / to)

6. There is a fire extinguisher system for use .... a fire in the laboratory.
   (of / event / the / unlikely / in)

7. It's my opinion that .... many further developments in the field of genetics.
   (undoubtedly / be / will / there)

8. It .... life will be found on other planets.
   (improbable / me / seems / to / that / highly)

The environment

☑ Exam task

🔊 Track 10 **You will hear five short extracts in which people are talking about the environment. For questions 1–5, choose from the list (A–H) what each speaker enjoys about what they do to look after the environment.**

A	learning from mistakes
B	getting support from others
C	feeling free of bad habits
D	meeting new people
E	persuading others to do something similar
F	avoiding extra expenses
G	making it part of a routine
H	staying informed about the subject

Speaker 1   **1** ☐

Speaker 2   **2** ☐

Speaker 3   **3** ☐

Speaker 4   **4** ☐

Speaker 5   **5** ☐

For questions 6–10, choose from the list (A–H) how each speaker feels about global environmental issues.

A	unsure what needs to be done
B	critical of some political policies
C	doubtful that things will change
D	annoyed by the attitude of the media
E	uneasy about approaches being taken
F	frustrated by the current state of affairs
G	disappointed by broken promises
H	convinced that things are improving

Speaker 1   **6** ☐

Speaker 2   **7** ☐

Speaker 3   **8** ☐

Speaker 4   **9** ☐

Speaker 5   **10** ☐

☑ Exam facts

- In this part, students listen to five monologues on a related topic.
- There are two multi-matching tasks, with each one focussing on a different aspect of what the speakers say.

2 Choose the correct preposition, a, b or c, to complete the sentences.

1. The committee is enquiring .... the effects of pesticides on human health.

   a over   **b** into   **c** against

2. You must have heard .... the book *Sustainable Energy: Without the Hot Air* – it's essential reading on environmental issues.

   a from   **b** by   **c** of

3. People have been arguing for years .... who should pay for cleaning up the environment.

   a about   **b** with   **c** against

4. If all the world's leaders could agree .... take decisive action, we might be able to save the planet.

   a with   **b** for   **c** to

5. All my friends advised me .... buying a car that uses a lot of fuel.

   a for   **b** to   **c** against

6. The future of tomorrow's environment depends .... the actions we take today.

   a on   **b** from   **c** of

7. All the evidence on climate change points .... it being the result of human activity.

   a about   **b** to   **c** over

8. We need to decide .... a clear policy to help reduce carbon emissions.

   a on   **b** into   **c** over

3 Complete the sentences with the most suitable word from the box.

bit	board	drive	go	grips	line	respect	said	trouble	wake

1. There's a thin .... between economic growth and unsustainable development.

2. It's going to .... you mad when you read this report about waste in the ocean.

3. Companies need to take on .... the views of the public about pollution.

4. Many people believe that boosting economic growth and tackling climate change should .... hand in hand.

5. People need to .... up to the fact that we're all responsible for looking after our planet.

6. Everybody has to do their .... to reduce their carbon footprint.

7. The future must lie in developing renewable sources of power. In that .... , solar energy needs much more investment.

8. Tackling the world's environmental problems is easier .... than done.

9. The government hasn't yet got to .... with the scale of the problem.

10. If we all took the .... to recycle more, there'd be far less waste.

Entertainment

☑ Exam task

1 🔊 **Track 11 You will hear five short extracts in which people are talking about working as actors. For questions 1–5, choose from the list (A–H) what has helped the speaker to succeed.**

A a calm personality

B a willingness to take risks   Speaker 1   **1** ☐

C an understanding of other people   Speaker 2   **2** ☐

D a lack of self-consciousness   Speaker 3   **3** ☐

E a love of music   Speaker 4   **4** ☐

F an ability to attract people   Speaker 5   **5** ☐

G an ability to be patient

H a constant wish to improve skills

For questions 6–10, choose from the list (A–H) what each speaker regrets about the past.

A studying the wrong subject

B deciding on a career too quickly   Speaker 1   **6** ☐

C being over-critical of others   Speaker 2   **7** ☐

D choosing an unsuitable first job   Speaker 3   **8** ☐

E mixing with unambitious people   Speaker 4   **9** ☐

F turning down a good offer of work

G being too competitive   Speaker 5   **10** ☐

H having fun instead of studying

2 **Match the adjectives 1–9 to their definitions a–i.**

1. uncomfortable	a having a personality that attracts people
2. devastated	b finding it easy and enjoyable to be with others
3. outgoing	c slightly embarrassed or awkward
4. single-minded	d very determined to achieve something
5. magnetic	e very shocked and upset
6. ruthless	f having extreme or strong emotions
7. modest	g putting a lot of effort into one's work
8. intense	h not worried about causing pain to others
9. conscientious	i not showing off one's abilities and achievements

3 Complete the sentences with the correct form of the verb in brackets.

1. I wish I .... so much of my time when I was training to be an actor. (not waste)

2. If only the director Jodorowsky .... the opportunity to make more movies before his death. (have)

3. Although he's a great guitarist, he often wishes he .... better. (can / sing)

4. I wonder if Al Pacino regrets .... a major role in the film *Star Wars*. (turn down)

5. The critic Nora Jewell should .... more generous in what she wrote about the play. It was so much better than her review suggested. (be)

6. If I .... acting as a career, I might have been a lawyer. (not / choose)

7. Do you have any regrets about .... your hand at directing a film? (not / try)

8. If there had been more opportunities for female directors in the past, the history of Hollywood .... very differently. (turn out)

Events and issues

☑ Exam task

1 🔊 Track 12 You will hear five short extracts in which people are talking about taking part in a public event. For questions 1–5, choose from the list (A–H) what each speaker feels about what they are doing.

A   relieved about the costs involved

B   happy to give up free time   Speaker 1   **1** ⬚

C   surprised at the amount of preparation   Speaker 2   **2** ⬚

D   confident about being successful   Speaker 3   **3** ⬚

E   pleased by the media attention

F   keen for it to be finished   Speaker 4   **4** ⬚

G   grateful for the help received   Speaker 5   **5** ⬚

H   determined to do it again

For questions 6–10, choose from the list (A–H) each speaker's main reason for taking part.

A   to avoid a sense of wasting time

B   to obtain a better job   Speaker 1   **6** ⬚

C   to practise a skill   Speaker 2   **7** ⬚

D   to surprise a friend

E   to prove a point   Speaker 3   **8** ⬚

F   to learn more about something   Speaker 4   **9** ⬚

G   to show off a talent   Speaker 5   **10** ⬚

H   to meet important people

Get it right!

Look at the sentences below. Then try to correct the mistake.

Empolyers won't accept those excuses, and to be honest, I won't accept them neither.

2 ▸ Complete the sentences with the correct words from the boxes.

demonstrating	seeking out	simplifying	socialising

1. This article about nuclear physics will need .... if ordinary people are to understand it.

2. Marta began her talk by .... just how much the population has grown using graphs.

3. Politicians have to spend a lot of time .... with important people if they want to have influence.

4. By .... people with the appropriate experience you might learn more than from sitting at your desk.

drafting	campaigning	covering	observing

5. James spent part of his degree in South America .... how climate change affects wild birds.

6. Luke is very involved in .... to improve healthcare for the elderly in his area.

7. The journalist .... the floods in the south of the country was exceptionally well-informed.

8. I always start a report by .... the main points and examples I want to include before actually writing it in detail.

3 ▸ Complete the conditional sentences with the correct form of the verbs from the box.

avoid	be (×2)	do	draw	have
	talk	try		

1. Unless something .... to prevent future flooding, the same problem will arise again.

2. If the media were .... more attention to the issue, people might give it more importance.

3. The meeting will continue for a further 20 minutes, so long as there .... any objections to this.

4. Provided you .... too much about the problems but focus on the solutions, I think your talk will go well.

5. Social inequality and injustice will continue unless more people .... access to a decent education.

6. If it .... for the police arriving so quickly, the thieves could have got away.

7. Many people believe greater financial regulation is needed if another global economic crisis is ....

8. If the government .... to create more employment opportunities, there is a greater danger of social unrest.

Education and learning

1a Complete each question using the correct form of a word from the boxes. Use each word once.

chance	opportunity	possibility	prospect

1. Do you have many .... to practise your English where you live?
2. What do you think your .... are of passing the Advanced exam?
3. Do you know that there is a .... that there might be three candidates in your Advanced speaking test?
4. Do you relish the .... of the exam day or are you dreading it?

important	particular	significant	unique

5. Do you think you need to work on any areas of your English in .... ?
6. How .... is it to be very familiar with the format of the exam do you think?
7. Do a .... number of people take the Advanced exam in your country?
8. Would you say that you have had a .... opportunity to do something? If so, what was it?

1b How would you answer questions 1–8 in exercise 1a? Try and say two to four sentences in reply to each of the questions.

2a 🔊 Track 13 Match the candidate's answers to the examiner's questions. Then listen and check.

Examiner

1. What is your favourite free-time activity at the moment?
2. What sort of work would you most like to do in the future?
3. If you had the opportunity, would you take a year out and travel?
4. What sort of things do you enjoy learning?
5. Do you like to give yourself aims and targets?
6. Are you planning to do any courses in the near future?

Candidate

a That would be fantastic! Of course, I'd need to save up beforehand. And maybe I'd need to do some work to survive financially. As I love discovering new places, it would be right up my street!

b Well, I'm studying economics, so I guess I'd prefer something related to finance. Perhaps banking or accounting.

c Right now, I'm just hoping to pass this exam! Once I've finished, I suppose I might take up another language. I quite fancy that.

d Currently, I prefer to do outdoor activities, like hiking or jogging. I try and keep myself fit. Sometimes I go alone and other times with friends.

e It depends. I have work ambitions, but outside work I like to take each day as it comes.

f When studying, I generally prefer figures to letters, but I do enjoy a good history book. And I find documentaries intriguing.

2b Now answer questions 1–6 so they are true for you.

✓ Exam fact

In this part, you talk about yourself and things you are interested in to show your ability to use general and social English.

© Cambridge University Press and UCLES 2016

✓ Exam task

3a 🔊 **Track 14 Put the words in order to make examiner's questions. Then listen and check.**

1. activity / most / do / what / free-time / enjoy / you ?

....

2. work / future / do / like / to / what / would / sort / you / of / the / in ?

....

3. take / if / opportunity / travel / you / year / had / you / a / would / out / to / the ?

....

4. learning / sort / do / what / enjoy / things / you / of ?

....

5. ideal / your / job / would / be / what ?

....

6. planning / do / near / courses / any / in / are / to / the / future / you ?

....

7. you / new / meet / where / live / easy / you / it / for / people / how / is / to ?

....

8. interest / about / find / you / out / that / do / you / things / how ?

....

3b 🔊 **Track 14 Listen again to the questions and answer them. Try and use phrases from the box below in your answers.**

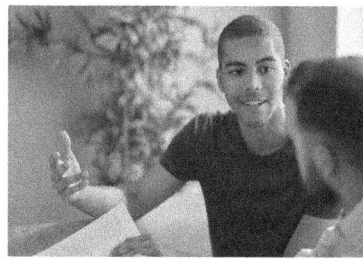

> I'd rather …   If I had the choice, I'd …
> I love …   I'm (not) suited to …   I most enjoy …
> I prefer … to …   I'd prefer …

Arts and entertainment

1 Read questions 1–8. Match the <u>underlined</u> idioms to the correct definitions a–h. Discuss the questions in pairs.

1. Which singers or actors that you know have <u>made a splash</u> recently? What did they do to attract so much attention?
2. Which place can you think of that has suddenly been <u>put back on the map</u>?
3. Would you say that you <u>have what it takes</u> to cope with being famous?
4. Are you <u>on the same wavelength</u> as anyone in your family?
5. Have you ever <u>bitten off more than you could chew</u>?
6. Which person on TV do you think really <u>knows their stuff</u>?
7. Would you say that you <u>have an ear for</u> music?
8. Do you still need to <u>put the finishing touches to</u> something you've made or written?

a Have the necessary qualities or talents to do something.
b Be very knowledgeable about a subject.
c Share very similar tastes and opinions.
d Suddenly become suddenly very famous or well-known.
e Try to do something that is too difficult or involves too much work.
f To do the final work or add the final improvements to something so that it's complete or satisfactory.
g Make somewhere or something become popular again.
h Be naturally good at understanding and picking up sounds.

2 Choose the correct verb form for each of these sentences.

It **(1)** *is / will be* time to announce a preview of our programmes for the upcoming season, which **(2)** *kicks / is kicking* off this Friday at 9 p.m. with the premiere of the new comedy series, *Split.* If you **(3)** *like / are liking* suspense, **(4)** *you'll love / you'll be loving* the serial drama, *Damage,* which **(5)** *will be broadcast / will have been broadcast* over four nights next week. In ten days' time, **(6)** *we're showing / we'll be showing* the long-awaited thriller – *Underground.* No doubt this classic **(7)** *is continuing / will continue* to keep you glued to your screen. Amazing to think that by November, we **(8)** *will watch / will have been watching Underground* for eight years! Further programmes **(9)** *are / are going* likely to be confirmed shortly, so sign up to receive updates and remember to bookmark your favourites!

☑ *Exam task*

🔊 **Track 15 Put the words in order to make the examiner's questions. Then listen and check.**

1. think / time / you / five / do / what / you / in / will / doing / year's / be ?

....

2. always / will / remember / which / you / teacher ?

....

3. week / you / on / to / are / watch / going / TV / what / this ?

....

4. by / what / 60 / to / you / hope / have / the / achieved / do / time / you're ?

....

5. at / the / interesting / recently / anything / cinema / have / you / seen ?

....

6. who / same / how / interests / as / important / have / is / to / it / friends / share / the / you ?

....

7. of / the / what / year / is / best / country / visit / time / to / your ?

....

8. to / you / do / find / easy / it / relax ?

....

3b **In pairs, ask and answer the questions in exercise 3a.**

☑ *Exam tips*

- Answer the examiner's questions promptly and naturally. Don't pause too long to think about your answers.
- Make your answers appropriate in length. Avoid answers of one or two words but don't give long and detailed answers.
- Try and use a variety of tenses, structures and vocabulary.

Travel

1 **Complete the sentences with the words in the box.**

excursions	journey	tour	travels	trip	visits	voyage

After their long plane **(1)** .... from Australia, the family are looking forward to their **(2)** .... of Scotland, which will include **(3)** .... to castles as well as **(4)** .... to landmarks like St Andrews. No doubt the real highlight for everyone will be the boat **(5)** .... on Loch Ness, where they hope to catch a glimpse of Nessie! Afterwards, they will board the cruise ship and set sail back home. This last **(6)** .... will take them more than six weeks. They hope to meet lots of interesting people during their **(7)** ....

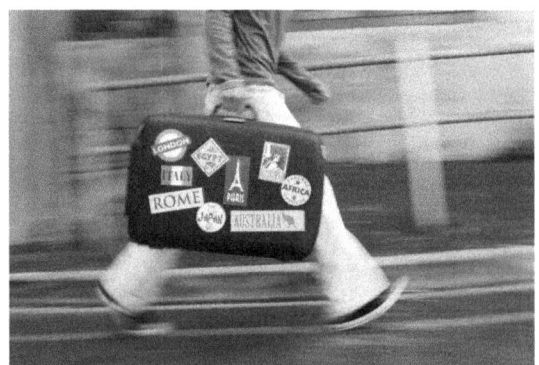

2 **Complete the questions with the correct verbs. Then answer the questions.**

1. What's the longest journey you've ever .... ?
2. If you could .... to any country in the world, where would you go?
3. How far do you have to walk from your home to .... a bus?
4. What was the last excursion you .... on?
5. Do you usually .... the escalator or the stairs?
6. When you go out for a walk, how many kilometres do you generally .... ?
7. Have you, or anyone you know, ever .... a sponsored swim or walk?
8. What things do you .... a lot of time doing when you're on holiday?

 Get it right!

Look at the sentence. Then try to correct the mistake.

In front of the metro station, there's a taxi rank, where probably you will find a taxi waiting.

3 Complete the sentences with a verb from the first box and a word expressing a degree of certainty from the second box.

could	may	might	will	won't

certainly	certainly not	most definitely	probably	probably not	possibly	undoubtedly

1. I .... have to speak in the Cambridge English Advanced Speaking Test.
2. There .... be one or two other candidates in the Speaking Test.
3. The next time I fly, I .... check in a suitcase.
4. The Olympic Games .... take place in my country in the next 20 years.
5. I .... have time to relax next weekend.
6. English .... be useful to me in the future.
7. Someday, people .... move to live on another planet.

✓ *Exam task*

4a 🔊 Track 16 Complete the examiner's questions and sentences with words from the box. Then listen and check your answers.

affect	celebrate	change	concerned	important	meet	wish	won

1. How do you think you might .... your next birthday?
2. Do you think we should live for today and not be .... about tomorrow?
3. How .... is being adventurous to you?
4. Which places are on your .... list?
5. If you could .... one thing about the area you live in, what would it be?
6. What would you do if you suddenly .... a lot of money?
7. Which famous person would you like to .... ?
8. If you were without internet for a week, how would it .... you?

4b In pairs, ask and answer the questions in exercise 4a.

Health and sport

1a Match 1–6 with a–f to make compound adjectives.

1. cross		a -breaking	
2. cutting		b -consuming	
3. last		c -country	
4. long		d -edge	
5. record		e -minute	
6. time		f -term	

1b Complete the sentences with the compound adjectives from exercise 1a.

1. The live event attracted a .... size of audience. Never before had so many spectators turned up on the day.

2. .... skiing is a fantastic way to explore snowy landscapes.

3. A considerable amount of time and money is spent on the design of .... sports equipment using the expertise of aeronautical engineers.

4. The moment you start exercising, you can feel its positive effects. .... benefits include a reduced risk of disease and increased life expectancy.

5. Training and preparing for a marathon is .... , exhausting and at times, very dull.

6. Disappointed fans missed seeing their heroes after the team suddenly announced a .... substitution of two of its players due to injury.

2 Correct the mistakes with the comparatives in the sentences.

1. Once the cause has been identified, doctors can prescribe the more suitable treatment.

....

2. The team's performance today was the most clear sign yet that they are back and ready to challenge the leaders.

....

3. The medical profession's bigest challenge is to deal with the shortage of nursing staff in rural areas.

....

4. Ticket sales were much more lower and slowlier than expected.

....

5. Tennis is the world's most favourite individual sport.

....

6. The city hospital is one of the bests in the country.

....

Exam task

3

 Track 17 Student A, compare two of the pictures and say how difficult it might be for the people to do these different activities, and what benefits people might get from doing these activities in groups.

Picture 1   Picture 2   Picture 3

Student B, which activity do you think would be the most enjoyable for the people involved?

Student B, compare two of the pictures and say why people might enjoy going to these events, and how difficult the events might be to organise.

Picture 4   Picture 5   Picture 6

Student A, which of these events do you think would attract the largest crowd?

Exam fact

- In this part, candidates speak without interruption to answer questions about two pictures out of a choice of three. They are also asked to comment about their partner's pictures.

© Cambridge University Press and UCLES 2016

Events and issues

1 **Complete the text with phrases from the box.**

a great deal	as far back	more straightforward	more extraordinary
more and more	much more thoughtful	less spontaneous	

Events, both personal and those which are **(1)** .... more public, can have a dramatic impact on our lives. Sometimes, for whatever reason, an everyday occurrence can suddenly stop us in our tracks and make us reflect or react. On other occasions, it is something far **(2)** .... that captures our attention and sticks in our minds.

Artists have been illustrating these effects and reactions for **(3)** .... as we have records. Cave paintings of birth, illness and death, together with contemporary photographs and sketches of war or disaster demonstrate the desire and the need to raise awareness of issues and events by illustrating them and leaving a record.

Thanks to the aid of technology, documenting and sharing events and reactions has become **(4)** .... immediate and considerably **(5)** .... A small plea: Could these reactions be **(6)** .... and slightly **(7)** .... (and edited!)?

2 **Complete the questions with the correct form of the verbs in the box.**

come	forward	keep	leave	print	raise	store	verify

1. Which events do you feel .... their mark on your life so far?

2. How do you .... a record of special events?

3. When you receive a message, photo or video which shows a reaction to an event, do you usually .... it to other people?

4. Do you ever check to see that something you have been sent or told really happened? How can we .... facts?

5. Which famous painting or photo .... to mind when we talk about recording an event and .... awareness?

6. With the use of mobile phones, ... photos and .... them in albums is nowhere near as common as it used to be.

 Exam tip

- Only talk about two of the pictures. Don't just describe them and make sure you answer both questions.

Exam task

3   Track 18 **Student A, compare two of the pictures and say why the people might have chosen to do these things together, and how the people might be feeling.**

Picture 1

Picture 2

Picture 3

Student B, which activity do you think needed the longest preparation?

Student B, compare two of the pictures and say why these people might be making these decisions, and how difficult it might be to make the decisions.

Picture 4

Picture 5

Picture 6

Student A, which decision do you think needs the most careful consideration?

Human creativity

1 Complete the text with an appropriate verb form from the box.

can (× 4)	could have been	may	may have been	may not
might	might have been	might not have	must be	

A masterpiece or fake?

Throughout history, works of art have been imitated and copied. Unfortunately, at times, they **(1)** .... forged. With vast amounts of money at stake, how **(2)** .... an investor tell if their purchase is genuine?

In the case of paintings, the details experts **(3)** .... decide to check include the age of the materials used (the pigments and canvas **(4)** .... of the kind used then); if the picture frame **(5)** .... changed; and whether the signature is genuine.

However, some artists **(6)** .... signed their works and signatures **(7)** .... easily be forged. Similarly, a full inventory of the works produced **(8)** .... exist.

Nowadays, of course, technology **(9)** .... be used to detect fraud. Via the internet, investigators **(10)** .... carry out research into a piece's history and forensic tests **(11)** .... reveal whether the materials present **(12)** .... used at the time of creation.

2 Look at the picture of people involved in an activity. Answer the questions. Use modal verbs to speculate.

1. How old do you think the children are?
2. How well do they know each other?
3. Where are they?
4. Are they alone or are there other people in the room?
5. What are they doing?
6. What are they supposed to be doing?
7. How long have they been here?
8. What will happen next?

 Get it right!

Look at the sentences below. Then try and correct the mistake.

'Do you see the baby foxes?' I asked. Thomas was very excited and he said, 'Yes, I see. But there must be their mother somewhere too.'

Exam task

3

🔊 Track 19 Student A, compare two of the pictures and say why the people might be making these things and what problems they might have.

Picture 1   Picture 2   Picture 3

Student B, which of these things might take the longest to make? Why?

Candidate B, compare two of the pictures and say why the people might be restoring these things and how patient they might need to be.

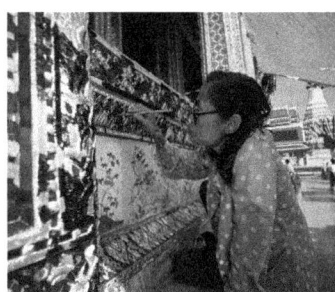

Picture 4   Picture 5   Picture 6

Candidate A, which of these things might be the most difficult to restore?

Psychology

1 **Match the definitions with the words in the box.**

| fear | insecurity | obsession | phobia | reaction | sympathetic | therapy | upset |

1. A treatment that helps a person grow stronger or feel better. ....
2. A word to describe a person who can relate to how another person is feeling and/or forgive them if they do something wrong. ....
3. Something or someone that you think about all the time. ....
4. An unpleasant emotion you feel when you are frightened. ....
5. Sad and/or worried. ....
6. A feeling of not being safe or confident. ....
7. A form of behaviour or feeling in response to an event or situation. ....
8. An extreme (and sometimes irrational) dislike or fear of a particular thing. ....

2 **Complete the sentences with your own ideas.**

1. An obvious example of our lack of personal privacy online is ....
   ....

2. We can support people who are suffering in many ways, for instance, by ....
   ....

3. It's vital to set aside time every day to do things such as ....
   ....

4. Sometimes parents do nothing to control their children's behaviour. A case in point is ....
   ....

5. Spending time with your family is really important. We can do this in various ways. One way to do this is ....
   ....

6. Having a down-to-earth approach to life is important. By this, what I mean to say is ....
   ....

7. Living mindfully includes living in the present. In other words, ...

3a 🔊 Track 20 **Here are some things that can affect our mood and a question for you to discuss.**

exercise — **How can these things affect our mood?** — the people we're with

music — the weather

our lifestyle

Talk to each other about how these different things can affect our mood. Then decide which of these things you think the most affects people's moods.

3b 🔊 Track 21 **Listen to the examiner's questions and take turns answering them.**

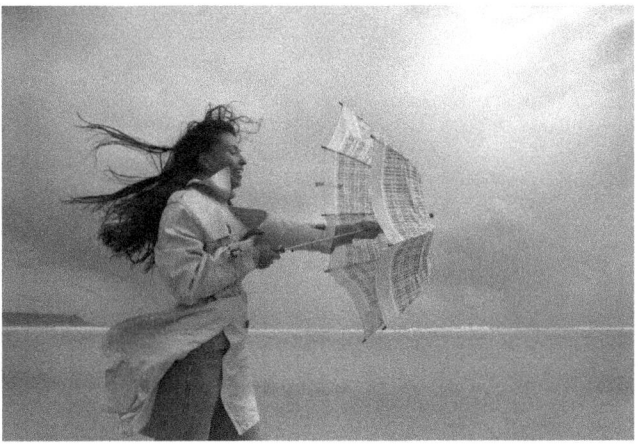

✓ **Exam facts**

- In Part 3, you perform two tasks with a partner. The first task is answering a central question with the help of prompts. In the second task, you are asked to make a decision related to what you discussed in the first task.
- In Part 4, you are asked additional questions to broaden the discussion in Part 3. This focusses on more abstract issues.

© Cambridge University Press and UCLES 2016

The environment

1 **Rewrite the sentences using the words in brackets to make them less direct. You may need to make some minor changes.**

1. You're right. (may well) ....

2. The best solution is for rubbish to be collected more frequently. (could be) ....
....

3. I would like to suggest an alternative. (just) ....

4. It's difficult to choose. (sort of) ....

5. Could you give more details? (I wonder if) ....

6. I agree. (tend to) ....

7. That is not the case. (necessarily) ....

8. Temperatures are rising. (It may be argued that) ....
....

2a **Complete the sentences with the words in the box.**

disagree	fair	far	look	more	see	sure	totally	way	wouldn't

1. That's a .... point.

2. I .... agree.

3. I .... what you mean.

4. I couldn't agree ....

5. I'm not .... I agree with you.

6. I'm afraid I have to .... with you here.

7. But .... you say that . . .

8. The .... I see things, . . .

9. The way I .... at it, . . .

10. As .... as I'm concerned, . . .

2b **Answer the questions using the expressions in 2a.**

1. The countryside is by far the best place to live. What do you think?

2. The damage to the environment is irreversible. Do you agree?

3. Most forest fires are caused by humans and could be prevented. What's your opinion?

4. Weather forecasts nowadays are more reliable than ever before. Wouldn't you agree?

5. Many more species of plants and animals will be discovered in our lifetime. What are your thoughts on this?

6. Switching off our phones and laptops for a whole day per week would be good for everyone and for the planet too. How do you feel about this idea?

3a 🔊 Track 22 **Here are some things that we can do to help the environment and a question for you to discuss.**

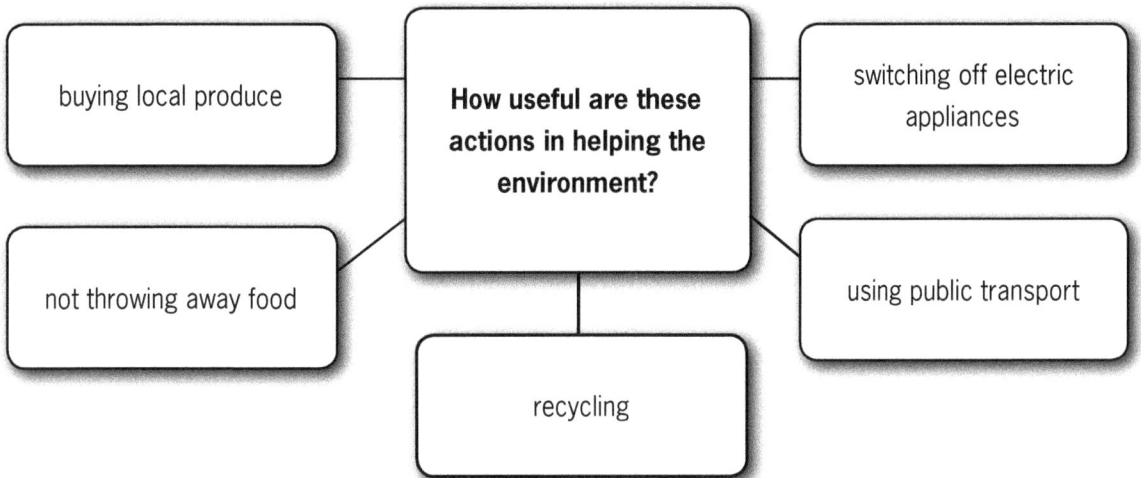

buying local produce

How useful are these actions in helping the environment?

switching off electric appliances

not throwing away food

using public transport

recycling

Talk to each other about how useful these actions are in helping the environment. Then decide which of these actions you think is the most important to do.

3b 🔊 Track 23 **Listen to the examiner's questions and take turns answering them.**

✓ **Exam tips**

- Use the reading time before you start speaking to understand the task and to think of language that you could use.
- Remember, the point of this task is for you to share opinions with the other candidate(s). You should try and introduce new ideas, comment on your partner's points and develop the interaction.
- Do not worry if you and the other candidate(s) do not reach a decision about the final question you are asked to discuss. You will not be penalised.

Work

1a **Match the two halves of the sentence starts.**

1. Wouldn't you agree	**a** mean, but . . .
2. You have a point, but the	**b** well, but . . .
3. I can see what you	**c** and good. However, . . .
4. That's all very	**d** that . . .
5. That's all well	**e** admit that . . .
6. If I can just say	**f** fact of the matter is that . . .
7. Yes. But you have to	**g** something here.

1b **Write responses to the opinions using phrases from exercise 1a. Use each phrase only once.**

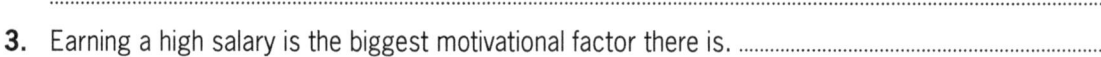

1. Anyone can multitask. You never need to only concentrate on one thing at once. ....

    ....

2. School does not prepare you for the real world. ....

    ....

3. Earning a high salary is the biggest motivational factor there is. ....

    ....

4. After a long day at work, the last thing you want to do is go to an evening class. ....

    ....

5. Becoming rich and famous is everyone's aim in life. ....

    ....

6. Working for a large company gives you far more opportunities than working for a small firm.

    ....

7. There comes a point when everyone would like to give up work and stay at home. ....

    ....

 Get it right!

Look at the sentences below. Then try to correct the mistake.

We want to build a school and a playground. Nevertheless we want to build shops near the new houses.

2 Write suitable first sentences and link them to 1–6 using concluding phrases from the box.

all things considered	at the end of the day	in conclusion	on balance
to conclude	to sum up	when all's said and done	

1. ....

   anyone can multitask. You never need to only concentrate on one thing at once.

2. ....

   school does not prepare you for the real world.

3. ....

   earning a high salary is the biggest motivational factor there is.

4. ....

   after a long day at work, the last thing you want to do is go to an evening class.

5. ....

   becoming rich and famous is everyone's aim in life.

6. ....

   working for a large company gives you far more opportunities than working for a small firm.

☑ **Exam task**

3a 🔊 Track 24 Here are some skills that people think are important for their working lives today and a question for you to discuss.

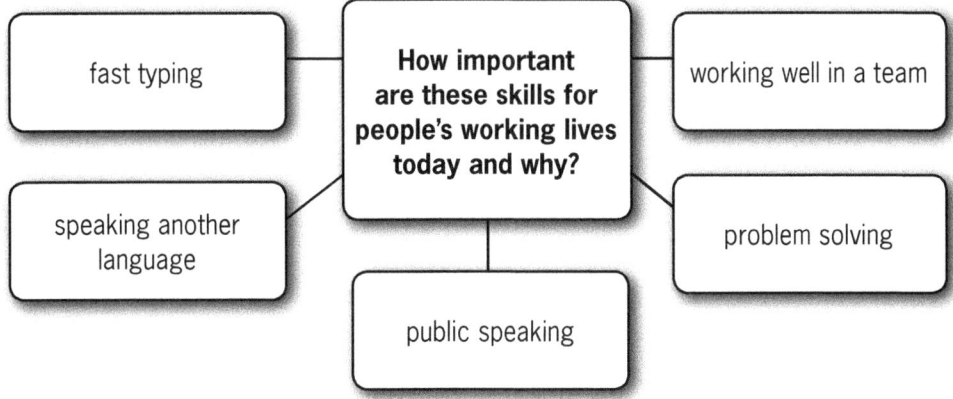

Talk to each other about how important these skills are for people's working lives today and why. Then decide which of these skills you think will be the most important to have in the future.

3b 🔊 Track 25 Listen to the examiner's questions and take turns answering them.

Think about it   Advanced Reading and Use of English Part 1

Read the sentences about Advanced Reading and Use of English Part 1. Are they TRUE or FALSE?

1. You read a text and answer questions about it. ....

2. The text is similar in length to Parts 2 and 3 of this Paper. ....

3. The first gap is already completed and is the example. ....

4. There are ten gaps to complete. ....

5. You have to choose from four options to fill each gap. ....

6. This part tests your lexical knowledge. ....

7. Most of the gaps are missing one word, but there may also be a short phrase missing. ....

8. Sometimes, more than one answer may be correct. ....

9. You have to write the missing word(s) on the separate answer sheet. ....

10. You get one mark for every correct answer. ....

Think about it   Advanced Reading and Use of English Part 2

Complete the text about Advanced Reading and Use of English Part 2 by writing one word in each gap.

Part 2 consists **(1)** .... a text in which there are nine gaps (the first **(2)** .... is an example). You have to complete the text by writing **(3)** .... one word in each gap.

The missing words **(4)** .... either grammatical, such **(5)** .... articles, auxiliaries, prepositions, pronouns; **(6)** .... lexico-grammatical, for example, phrasal verbs and words within fixed phrases.

The answer will **(7)** .... be a single word. In some **(8)** .... , there may be more than one possible answer and **(9)** .... is allowed for in the mark scheme.

Spelling, as in **(10)** .... parts of the Use of English component, must be correct.

Think about it — Advanced Reading and Use of English Part 3

Choose the correct alternative to complete the text about Advanced Reading and Use of English Part 3.

In Part 3, you have to read **(0)** *sentences / a text* and complete **(1)** *it / them*, using **(2)** *one word / between three and six words*. There is **(3)** *no / an* example and then there are **(4)** *8 / 10* gaps to fill.

The **(5)** *word / words* that you need to write **(6)** *is / are* formed from the word which appears at the **(7)** *start / end* of the line.

You might need to add a prefix to the **(8)** *start / end* of that word, to add a suffix to the **(9)** *start / end* of it, as well as perhaps other, internal changes. Remember that suffixes often indicate the tense of a verb, or change the word class (e.g. *real → realise* or *real → reality*).

You have to write your answers on the answer sheet and you should do this in **(10)** *CAPITAL / lowercase* letters.

You should check the spelling of all the words you write **(11)** *carefully / carelessly* because it must be correct.

Think about it — Advanced Reading and Use of English Part 4

Match 1–8 to a–h to make sentences about Advanced Reading and Use of English Part 4.

1. Part 4 consists of
2. Each question contains
3. You have to
4. The gap must be filled
5. The key word
6. The focus is on
7. A range
8. There are two marks

a   fill the gap in the second sentence.

b   both lexis and grammar.

c   six questions, plus one example.

d   of structures and lexis is tested.

e   using between three and six words.

f   three parts: a lead-in sentence, a key word and a second sentence of which only the beginning and end are given.

g   available for each question and you might get one of the marks if part of your answer is correct.

h   must not be changed in any way.

Think about it   Advanced Reading and Use of English Part 5

Read the statements about Advanced Reading and Use of English Part 5. Are they TRUE or FALSE?

1. There are three options to choose from (**A**, **B** or **C**) for each question. ....

2. There are six questions in total for this part of the exam. ....

3. Part 5 tests the ability to understand and identify both content and organisation of complex texts.

   ....

4. The texts are between 700 and 800 words.

5. It is common for Part 5 to contain questions about the writer's opinion or attitude. ....

6. In Part 5, you may have to identify the correct order of the different sections of text. ....

7. Some of the questions in Part 5 may test implied meaning that is not directly stated in the text.

   ....

8. The texts in Part 5 could be book extracts, newspaper or magazine articles, reviews, or from specialist journals. ....

 Think about it   Advanced Reading and Use of English Part 6

Match 1–8 with a–h to make sentences about Advanced Reading and Use of English Part 6.

1. In Part 6, candidates must read across different texts in order to

2. Across the four texts,

3. The four texts could be

4. Reading across four texts in this way and analysing, comparing and contrasting information

5. The questions that are asked for Part 6 of the Advanced Reading exam

6. There may be questions about which writer

7. There may be questions about one writer

8. Each question is about a different sub-topic

a reviews or extracts from articles.

b are of three types.

c agrees or disagrees with another writer.

d there is a total of 550–600 words.

e who expresses a different opinion to the other three writers.

f find relevant information about the other writers.

g and writers give their opinions on some or all of these.

h is an important academic skill.

Think about it — Advanced Reading and Use of English Part 7

Read the text about the Advanced Reading and Use of English Part 7 and the following statements. Are the statements TRUE or FALSE?

Part 7 of the Advanced Reading and Use of English exam consists of a long text from which six paragraphs have been removed. The text can come from a wide variety of sources, such as articles and reviews. There are six numbered gaps marked in the text to show where the missing paragraphs go. The six paragraphs that have been removed appear alongside the main body of the text. To make things more difficult, the paragraphs are mixed up and an extra paragraph, which does not fit into any of the gaps, is added. This part of the exam tests candidates' awareness of how long texts are organised, and their ability to recognise how language is used to carefully link all the sections of a text together in a coherent way. To answer the questions, candidates write the letter of the paragraph they think fits in a gap next to the number of the gap. One of the missing paragraphs may be a long single sentence, but the others are all two or more sentences long. The overall text length is between 650 and 800 words, including the missing paragraphs. The main body of the text makes up about 60% of this word count, and the removed paragraphs around 40%.

1. The text for Part 7 is very long and is usually made up of six paragraphs. ....
2. The text is always an article or review. ....
3. There are six items to complete in this part of the test. ....
4. Paragraphs that have been removed are presented in random order. ....
5. There are six extra paragraphs added to the missing paragraphs to increase the difficulty. ....
6. Part 7 tests candidates' understanding of the structure of a long text. ....
7. Most of the removed paragraphs consist of one long sentence. ....
8. The paragraphs that have been removed contain about 650 words. ....

Think about it — Advanced Reading and Use of English Part 8

Complete the text about Advanced Reading and Use of English Part 8 using the correct words or phrases from the box.

letter	section	between 600 and 700 words	four to six
Part 6	ten questions	multiple matching	extracts

Part 8 of the Advanced Reading and Use of English exam is a **(1)** .... task. Candidates have to pair questions with a short text or a **(2)** .... from a longer text. There are three types of task. The first has **(3)** .... short texts usually written by different people about a single topic (which is similar in some ways to **(4)** .... of the exam). The second type is a long text split into four parts, A–D. The third type is made up of **(5)** .... taken from different sources about the same topic. In each case, the answer to each question is the **(6)** .... of the text or part of the text where the information is found. There are **(7)** .... to answer and the text or texts are **(8)** .... in total.

Think about it ▶ Advanced Writing Part 1

Match questions 1–6 about Advanced Writing Part 1 to answers a–f.

1. What do you have to write?

2. What do you have to write about?

3. What should you include?

4. How can you develop the given points?

5. How many words should you write?

6. What's a good way to organise your essay?

a   220–260.

b   Reasons and examples to support and illustrate your argument and make sure that you decide on one of your points clearly in your conclusion.

c   An essay.

d   Two of the three points you are given related to the topic.

e   An introduction, 2–3 paragraphs and a conclusion.

f   If you like, use some of the opinions provided to develop your points.

Think about it ▶ Advanced Writing Part 2

Write the missing numbers in the sentence about Advanced Writing Part 2.

In Advanced Writing Part 2, you have to choose **(1)** .... task from a choice of

(2) .... and write between **(3)** .... and **(4)** .... words.

Cross out the text types would NOT appear in Advanced Writing Part 2.

an article	a report	an email or letter	a review
	an essay	a story	a proposal

Complete the table with the text types.

email/letter   proposal   report   review

Text type	Layout, content and organisation
(5)	Will include factual information and make suggestions or recommendations. Clearly organised and will include headings.
(6)	Similar to report. Recommendations for course of action. Persuasive. Clearly organised and will use headings.
(7)	Will include description and explanation, positive and negative opinions and make a recommendation.
(8)	May be very formal or more informal. Will include factual information or describe a personal experience. Writing conventions (opening salutation, closing, clear paragraphing) should be used.

Think about it   Advanced Listening Part 1

Complete the text about Listening Part 1 with the correct words from the box.

agree	attitudes	detail	dialogue	multiple-choice	purpose	topics	total	three

In Part 1, you will listen to **(1)** .... short texts. Each text has two **(2)** .... questions

for you to answer. For each question, there are three options to choose from. There are six questions in

(3) .... to answer in Part 1.

Each text consists of a **(4)** .... between two speakers, and lasts about one minute. The texts will

cover a variety of possible **(5)** .... , and there will be different voices and styles of delivery. The

questions may test your understanding of the gist or **(6)** .... of what is said. The questions may

also test your understanding of what the speakers **(7)** .... or disagree about, the function or

(8) .... of what they say, their feelings, **(9)** .... and opinions.

     Think about it   Advanced Listening Part 2

Complete the text about Listening Part 2 with the correct words from the box.

audience	gap	monologue	order	phrase	specific	spelling	style	talk

In Part 2, you will hear a **(1)** .... , in which a single speaker talks for around three minutes. The

listening text may be a **(2)** .... , lecture or part of a broadcast, and will be aimed at a non-specialist

(3) .... The **(4)** .... of speech will be neutral or semi-formal. Part 2 tests your

ability to identify **(5)** .... information, and stated opinions.

The task consists of eight sentences, each with a **(6)** .... , where a piece of information is missing.

The missing information is contained in the recording that you will hear, and the sentences will come in the same

(7) .... as in the recording. You will have to write a single word or short **(8)** .... in

the gap. Your **(9)** .... should be correct, but both British and US forms are allowed.

Think about it   Advanced Listening Part 3

Read the information about Listening Part 3 and choose the correct word from the box for each space.

order	six	two	read	feelings	options
agree	three to four	detailed	purpose	discussing	interviewer

In Part 3, you will listen to an interview or discussion. There will usually be **(1)** .... speakers, who

will be **(2)** .... a topic. There may be a third speaker who is the **(3)** .... This person

asks the other speakers short questions. The audio text will last approximately **(4)** .... minutes.

You will have **(5)** .... multiple-choice questions to answer. Each question has four

(6) .... The questions appear in the same **(7)** .... as the information given in

the recording.

The questions will test your ability to understand the speakers' attitudes and opinions. The questions may focus on

(8) .... and gist understanding, and also the speaker's attitudes, opinions and

(9) .... , or whether they **(10)** .... about something. Questions may also deal with

the **(11)** .... or function of what a speaker says.

Before you listen to the recording for the first time, you will have 70 seconds to **(12)** .... through

the questions. You will hear the recording twice.

 Think about it   Advanced Listening Part 4

Complete the text with the correct words from the box.

choose	extra	match	order	speaker	theme	twice	use

Part 4 is a multiple matching task. You will hear five monologues about a particular **(1)** .... or

topic. Each of the five texts will have a different **(2)** .... , and will last approximately 30 seconds.

There are two tasks, each one consisting of eight options to **(3)** .... from. You will have to

(4) .... the correct option to each speaker for Task 1 and Task 2. There are also three

(5) .... options in each task that you will not need to **(6)** .... You will hear the

series of monologues **(7)** .... , but you can do the tasks in any **(8)** ....

Think about it Advanced Speaking Part 1

Read the tips and tick ✓ the tips which are good advice for things to do in Part 1 of the Advanced Speaking Test.

1. Take time to think about your answers before you speak. ....

2. Give short answers (1–4 words) to the examiner's questions. ....

3. It's good to prepare some of your answers and learn them by heart. ....

4. If you don't understand or haven't heard something, ask the examiner to repeat it. ....

5. You should turn and talk to the other candidate(s) and involve them in a conversation in Part 1. ....

6. Try and use a range of verb tenses in this part of the exam. ....

7. Don't try and use language that you are not 100% sure of. Stick to simple words. ....

8. For questions that you have never been asked or thought about before, there are some useful phrases to give yourself thinking time that you can learn and practise using. ....

Think about it Advanced Speaking Part 2

Match 1–7 with a–g to make sentences about Advanced Speaking Part 2.

1. In Part 2, you will have to speak for

2. You should answer two questions which the examiner asks you and are printed

3. The three pictures are connected in some way

4. A good approach to this part is to

5. Your partner will answer

6. The other candidate will also speak for a minute to answer

7. You will also have to give a short answer (about 30 seconds)

a and the examiner will mention this connection when they give you the sheet with the pictures.

b one minute about two pictures.

c above the three pictures which you are given.

d a short question related to the pictures that you have described.

e start by comparing the pictures and then move on to answering the two questions above the pictures.

f about your partner's pictures so make sure you look at them and listen to what your partner says!

g two questions about another set of pictures.

Complete the text about Advanced Speaking Parts 3 and 4 using words from the box. Use each word once only.

| broaden | discussed | explaining | focus | giving | look | make | refer | tells | telling |

In Part 3, the examiner will give you some spoken instructions, **(1)** .... you that you should talk to

the other candidate for about two minutes and **(2)** .... briefly the theme of the discussion before

(3) .... you a sheet to look at.

On the sheet, there are some written prompts and a central question. You will have about 15 seconds to

(4) .... at these before the examiner **(5)** .... you what to talk about in relation to

the prompts.

After you and your partner have **(6)** .... this first question, the examiner will ask you to

(7) .... a decision related to the prompts you have just been discussing. You are not assessed on

your ability to reach an agreement.

In Part 4, the examiner will ask questions to **(8)** .... the topics introduced in Part 3. The questions

often **(9)** .... on more abstract issues, especially as the discussion continues. In this part,

you can and should interact with your partner and comment on and **(10)** .... the points that

they have mentioned. Do not, however, interrupt them abruptly before they have finished and avoid dominating

the conversation.

ANSWER KEY

Reading and Use of English Part 1:1

1 1 orchestra   2 stage   3 compilation
4 exhibition   5 choir   6 skills
7 bill   8 camera

2 1 are
2 are giving / give
3 are
4 are staying
5 books
6 take
7 head / are heading
8 make
9 kick off
10 rest / are resting
11 hit
You can use the present simple for all answers except 4.

3 1 C   2 D   3 C   4 B   5 A   6 C   7 B   8 D

Reading and Use of English Part 1:2

1 1 A   2 B   3 D   4 C   5 B   6 C   7 A   8 B

2 1 find, tricky   2 make, happy
3 considers /considered, fortunate
4 kept / keeps, busy   5 call, perfect

3 1 latest, Last, previous
2 common, regular, normal
3 long, big, wide
4 significant, large, great
5 distant, far, remote
6 different, unique, varied

4 1 talk   2 learn   3 convince
4 introducing   5 express   6 treated
7 know

Reading and Use of English Part 1:3

1 1 on   2 for   3 against   4 for
5 for   6 in   7 of   8 to

2 1 occasions   2 incidents   3 cases
4 examples   5 investigation   6 research
7 survey   8 enquiry   9 attraction
10 attention   11 focus   12 interest

3 1 D   2 B   3 A   4 C   5 C   6 C   7 D   8 B

Get it right!
For most of people it seems to be so natural – animals in cages.

Reading and Use of English Part 2:1

1 1 came into
2 come through
3 come under
4 come off
5 come up
6 came across
7 come between
8 coming down

2 1 both are correct
2 both are correct
3 b is wrong
4 b is wrong
5 both are correct
6 both are correct
7 b is wrong
8 a is wrong

3 1 YOURSELF/YOURSELVES   2 AT   3 FROM/BY
4 DO   5 PUT   6 IF/WHETHER   7 NOT
8 THANKS/DUE

Reading and Use of English Part 2:2

1 1 WHAT   2 WILL   3 WITH
4 A   5 AS   6 SAY
7 BECAUSE   8 ON/ABOUT

2 1 accounts   2 result   3 matter
4 words   5 happens   6 First
7 time   8 now

3 1 Has your personal experience of studying (-) science subjects at (-) school been **a** positive one?
2 How far would you say that (-) science fulfils **a** useful role in (-) modern society?
3 Which discovery or invention do you think has had **the** most positive effect on (-) society?
4 How do you think (-) medicine will develop in future?
5 How strict do you think **the**/(-) controls on (-) scientific experiments should be?
6 To what extent are (-) human beings to blame for (-) climate change?
7 Do you think that (-) advances in (-) technology will be sufficient to overcome **the** problem of **the** world's dwindling resources?
8 Some people say that **the** more we invent, **the** lazier we become.

Reading and Use of English Part 2:3

1 1 coastal erosion
2 oil spill
3 rural areas
4 urban development
5 waste management
6 global warming
7 natural habitats
8 endangered species

2 1 eligible for
2 open-minded about, hostile to
3 prone to
4 restricted to
5 untouched by
6 lacking in
7 incompatible with

3 1 OF   5 WITH
2 SOME/MANY   6 BY
3 TO   7 NOT
4 SHOULD/COULD   8 WHO/THAT

Get it right!
Our town is really full of <u>tourist</u> attractions. I mean all these marvellous monuments.

Reading and Use of English Part 3:1

1 1 immature   5 misbehaviour
2 disorganised   6 Pre-booking
3 unconventional   7 undertaken
4 overcome   8 inconvenient

2
1 Why
2 (that)
3 when
4 where
5 who/that
6 whose
7 (which/that)
8 which

The pronouns that can be omitted are in brackets.

3
1 THEORETICAL
2 INDEPENDENTLY
3 DISSATISFACTION
4 COMPLAINTS
5 PROVIDERS
6 CLARIFY
7 ENSURE
8 UNREALISTIC/UNREAL

Reading and Use of English Part 3:2

1
1 GROWTH
2 INCREASINGLY
3 OCCURRENCE
4 ADJUSTMENTS
5 CONSIDERABLE
6 MATERIALISED/ MATERIALIZED
7 MANUFACTURERS
8 INCOME

2
1 unwillingness
2 significance
3 exaggeration
4 improvement
5 existence
6 necessity

3
1 The judges considering the evidence have all got a lot of experience.
2 Referees not giving their full attention to a match are a cause for concern.
3 The sports star featured in the article is said to be a millionaire.
4 The gymnasts competing in a range of events require strength, agility, flexibility and balance.
5 The golfer wearing the yellow jumper is the favourite to win the competition.
6 Anyone wanting to lose weight should diet and do exercise.
7 All the people selected for the experiment found it really interesting.
8 Keith Jones is not yet match fit, having undergone knee surgery less than a year ago.

Reading and Use of English Part 3:3

1 1 a 2 c 3 e 4 d 5 g 6 b 7 f

1b
1 hilarious/fabulous
2 insane
3 immense/enormous
4 devastated
5 pointless/senseless
6 fabulous/magnificent
7 appalling/disgusting

Get it right!

Every day we learn about <u>bad</u> habits we have in our daily lives and how they affect the environment.

2
1 MISHANDLING
2 HANDY
3 SECOND-HAND
4 CHANGEABLE
5 UNCHANGED
6 EXCHANGE/ INTERCHANGE
7 WORKOUT
8 HARDWORKING
9 TEAMWORK

3
1 REFLECTIONS
2 BASICS
3 PARTICULARLY
4 REINFORCED
5 RESTLESS
6 DEPTH
7 BROADENING
8 SURPRISINGLY

Reading and Use of English Part 4:1

1
1 signs   2 harm   3 thing
4 way   5 use   6 joke
7 surprise   8 wonder

2
1 At no point was there (ever) a mention of a conflict.
2 Never before had I come across the term 'mindfulness'.
3 Should you (ever) happen to see your former colleague, tell her was asking after her.
4 Hardly had the reunion begun when the fire alarm went off.
5 Not only do we eat more sugar and salt than our ancestors, but our diet also induces more acid.
6 Had I known how stubborn my teammate could be, I would never have tried to persuade him.
7 No sooner had I put forward the proposal than it was accepted.
8 Not only can providing role models for children inspire them to study, but it may also mean that they achieve more in life.

3
1 WERE OF NO **I CONSEQUENCE** TO
2 TO BE A **THOROUGH I** OVERHAUL OF
3 IS/CAN BE NO **I** DOUBT/QUESTION **WHATSOEVER**
4 O**NCE** WAS I **I** (EVER) ASKED TO
5 HAVEN'T A/THE SLIGHTEST **I CLUE** HOW / HAVE NOT/HAVEN'T GOT A **I CLUE** HOW / HAVE NO **I CLUE** HOW
6 HELD IN **I** SUCH (HIGH) **REGARD**

Reading and Use of English Part 4:2

1
1 on   2 under   3 from
4 behind   5 off   6 like
7 through/on   8 in

2
1 Apparently, the newspaper's market share stood at 35% in the first half of the year.
   The newspaper's market share apparently stood at 35% in the first half of the year.
2 To begin with, I was sceptical, but I think it's what the readership needed.
   I was sceptical to begin with, but I think it's what the readership needed.
3 By all accounts, the advent of the internet hit the greeting card industry hard.
   The advent of the internet hit the greeting card industry hard, by all accounts.
4 She will probably pursue a career in publishing.
   She will pursue a career in publishing, probably.

5 When it comes down to it, do you think that targeted direct mail really persuades us to purchase products?

Do you think that, when it comes down to it, targeted direct mail really persuades us to purchase products?

Do you think that targeted direct mail really persuades us to purchase products, when it comes down to it?

6 Needless to say, future issues of the magazine will be printed on recycled paper.

Future issues of the magazine will, needless to say, be printed on recycled paper.

3 1 KEEPS (HIMSELF)/ STAYS UP **I** TO **DATE** WITH
2 IT HADN'T/HAD NOT **I** BEEN **FOR** / IT WERE /WAS **I** 'NT/NOT **FOR**
3 IT **AMOUNTS** TO **I** IS THAT IT
4 CAME OUT **I** OF THE **BLUE**
5 **INCLINED** TO **I** AGREE WITH YOU
6 TOOK **ISSUE** **I** WITH THE (PRESS) COVERAGE

Reading and Use of English Part 4:3

1 1 brush up on
2 done away with
3 fits in … with
4 stay away from
5 get through to
6 stand up to
7 come up against

2 1 What forced the evacuation of hundreds of residents and the closure of the airport was the volcanic eruption.
It was the volcanic eruption that forced the evacuation of hundreds of residents and the closure of the airport.

2 What causes animals to be added to the list of endangered species is the destruction of the natural habitats.
It's the destruction of the natural habitats that causes animals to be added to the list of endangered species.

3 What never ceases to amaze me is the public response to large-scale disasters.
It's the public response to large-scale disasters that never ceases to amaze me.

4 What has led to a ban on hose pipes for the foreseeable future is the ongoing drought.
It's the ongoing drought that has led to the ban on hose pipes for the foreseeable future.

5 What flooded the roads and made the rivers burst their banks was the torrential rain.
It was the torrential rain that flooded the roads and caused rivers to burst their banks.

6 What is needed are more severe measures to tackle the issue of global warming.
It's more severe measures that are needed to tackle the issue of global warming.

3 1 **UNTIL** LAST FRIDAY THAT **I** REPRESENTATIVES WERE
2 CLAIMS WERE **I** **BACKED** UP
3 UNLESS/IF NO **STEPS** **I** ARE TAKEN TO / UNLESS WE TAKE **I** **STEPS** TO
4 **UTTERLY** AMAZING **I** WAS THE (SPECTACULAR)
5 YOU PUT/GET YOUR PROPOSAL **I** ACROSS **CLEARLY**
6 BE A MUCH/FAR **I** LESS COMMON **SIGHT**

Get it right!
I was very excited and I was looking forward to their arrival.

Reading and Use of English Part 5:1

1 1 B 2 C 3 D 4 B 5 A 6 C

2 1 pointing
4 worry
7 to find
2 Avoiding
5 joining
8 asking
3 to know
6 to watching

Reading and Use of English Part 5:2

1 1 B 2 C 3 A 4 C 5 D 6 B

2 1 Proposals are being considered to increase the number of bus routes.
2 It's said to be the most cosmopolitan city on the planet.
3 The mayor was told that more parks should be created.
4 The results of the poll will be published after the votes have been counted.
5 (They said that) nothing could be done until the rubbish had been cleared away.
6 The shopping centre was damaged after it had been broken into (by vandals).
7 A man was arrested after he had been stopped for driving too fast.
8 I have been asked to inform you that the next residents' meeting has been cancelled.

Reading and Use of English Part 5:3

1 1 D 2 B 3 C 4 C 5 A 6 D

2 1 has made
2 will have sold
3 had played
4 have been studying
5 have tried
6 had been downloading
7 had read
8 will have finished/ have got

Get it right!
Dear Alex, I am happy to have received a letter from you.

Reading and Use of English Part 6:1

1 1 A 2 C 3 D 4 B

2 1 b 2 a 3 b 4 a 5 b 6 b 7 a 8 a

Reading and Use of English Part 6:2

1 1 A 2 B 3 D 4 B

2 1 so   2 such   3 too
   4 enough   5 as, result   6 therefore
   7 too   8 such

Reading and Use of English Part 6:3

1 1 B 2 C 3 C 4 D

2 1 famous for   5 worried about
   2 capable of   6 furious with
   3 involved in   7 astonished by
   4 opposed to   8 keen on

Get it right!
The further education sector is much bigger <u>than</u> the university sector in the UK.

Reading and Use of English Part 7:1

1 1 F 2 B 3 G 4 E 5 A 6 C Distractor: D

2 1 had been demanding
   2 will have been
   3 have traded
   4 will have been continuously growing
   5 has often considered
   6 had been rising
   7 might have invented / had been
   8 had been invested / would have been developed

Reading and Use of English Part 7:2

1 1 D 2 A 3 F 4 C 5 G 6 B Distractor: E

2 1 about 340 kg in weight
   2 increase in the number of microwaves
   3 no indication that domestic microwaves pose a risk to health
   4 still has (great) relevance
   5 more investment (by companies) in finding
   6 very slow (public) acceptance of
   7 in (great) poverty

Reading and Use of English Part 7:3

1 1 G 2 C 3 E 4 A 5 F 6 D Distractor: B

2 1 get/have their college fees paid
   2 got her revision done
   3 got/had my letter of application typed
   4 was having/was getting his hair cut
   5 had had the number of drama classes reduced
   6 got the exhibition trip subsidised
   7 has had its funding increased
   8 getting/having my costume cleaned

Get it right!
The ladies <u>have their hair done</u>.

Reading and Use of English Part 8:1

1 1 had done   5 would be able
   2 go   6 will lose
   3 didn't have   7 would be
   4 will give   8 to find

2 1 B 2 C 3 D 4 A 5 C 6 A 7 D 8 B
   9 D 10 A

Reading and Use of English Part 8:2

1 1 f 2 d 3 a 4 h 5 g 6 c 7 b 8 e

2 1 B 2 C 3 B 4 D 5 A 6 C 7 B 8 D
   9 A 10 C

Reading and Use of English Part 8:3

1 1 C 2 A 3 D 4 B 5 A 6 C 7 B 8 D
   9 A 10 B

2 1 made   2 to take   3 gave
   4 have   5 to make   6 had done
   7 took   8 gave

Get it right!
If we think the club is boring, we should <u>do</u> something about it.

Writing Part 1:1

1 1 wounded   5 reaching
   2 beaten   6 gain
   3 earn   7 injured
   4 hurt   8 win

2 1 although (remove final 't')
   2 Nevertheless (one word)
   3 Neither/Nor
   4 Despite (spelling mistake – 'e' not 'i')
   5 Even though (two words)
   6 as/because
   7 than

3 1 eating well
   2 taking medicine
   3 diet, necessary nutrients, full range of foods which doctors recommend, feed, variety of healthy foods
   4 access to health care, supply of medicines, medical intervention, advances in medicine, drug treatments, illnesses, health problems, diseases, drugs, vaccines administered, bugs, immune, resistant, prescribed, medical scientists, cures, dosing, pills
   5 eating well

4 Model answer

It is widely accepted that sport benefits people. We all know that it is good for our physical health, but it also helps us in less obvious ways, in terms of our mental health and in creating healthy communities by building up a community spirit.

With regards to our mental health, sports often require a focus on an activity, for example hitting a ball or finding a foot hole in a rock face. This focus means we have to forget about whatever problems or emotions have been troubling us and concentrate on the activity we're involved in. It is hard to remember your negative emotions when you have to return a serve.

The focus on activity also helps us in team sports. Winning as a team is more important than how you feel about your fellow teammates. However, the value to building community spirit is usually because local people support their local teams. They feel inspired by local action. The team doesn't have to be professional for this to happen. In fact, it doesn't have to be a team sport. Local fun runs in aid of the local hospital or dads versus children football matches all bring people together.

Both aspects are important benefits of sport, but I think that probably community involvement provides the greatest benefit because it helps everyone not just those who are good at sports.

Writing Part 1:2

1a 1 case
   2 opinion/view
   3 seems
   4 knowledge
   5 fact
   6 As
   7 deny
   8 opinion/view

1b Possible answers
   1 It seems to be the case that **in poorer areas, many students drop out of school for financial reasons**.
   2 In my opinion/view, **many of the subjects we study at school do not prepare us for the real world**.
   3 It seems to me that **students are given far too much homework. They end up going to bed extremely late**.
   4 It is common knowledge that **many teachers struggle with new technologies and do not feel confident enough to use them in the classroom**.
   5 The fact is that **there is a sizeable shortage of skilled workers as fewer and fewer school leavers take up a trade**.
   6 As I see it, **having a good teacher who inspires you can make all the difference to your success later in life**.
   7 Few people would deny that **a good education can set you up for life**.

   8 In my opinion/view, **everyone should be made to learn to speak at least one foreign language**.

2 Possible answers
   1 Whenever you decide to learn something new, **make sure you are aware of how much time and dedication it will take**.
   2 Getting into university can be tough, yet **it is worth the effort**.
   3 Whichever subject you study, **a degree will provide useful skills and knowledge for the future**.
   4 However much you hate exams, **they are an unavoidable part of the education system**.
   5 Stress is bad for us, yet **at the same time, can be positive if experienced for just a short period**.
   6 No matter how much money you may make, **if you don't feel fulfilled in your job, you won't be happy**.
   7 Whatever happens at work, **try and not let it interfere with your personal life**.
   8 Wherever you end up working, **make sure you try and connect with the people around you**.

3 Model answer

We spend around eight hours a day in our workplaces, so having environments that are people friendly is very important for our health and well-being. Unfortunately, offices are too often harsh environments, with florescent lights, bare walls and unattractive views from the windows. However, there are things that can be done to improve things.

One of the easiest things to do is improve the way offices are decorated. Humans react to colours in either positive or negative ways, so painting the walls in colours that improve our mood and help make us feel cheerful towards others would be a great help. In addition, paintings or murals can make the walls look more interesting and reduce the bleakness of large areas of wall space.

In addition to improving the decoration, tackling poor light and ventilation helps people feel better. In gloomy offices where there is little fresh air, people often get frequent headaches and generally feel ill, so going to work becomes detrimental to their health. Day-light balanced bulbs and improved air circulation not only reduce these problems, but also increase workers' productivity.

Although improving all three factors is important, I think improving the light and ventilation are probably the most important, because the detrimental effect of poor light and poor air is more significant than the effect of looking at boring walls all day.

Writing Part 1:3

Possible answers (adverbs can go at front or end position)

1 1 Apparently, some thieves broke into the village shop last night.

2 Coincidentally, the police were doing their rounds when the break-in took place.

3 Fortunately, they were able to stop the robbers from stealing anything from the store.

4 Regrettably, a police officer was slightly injured when making the arrest.

5 Thankfully, her injuries are not thought to be serious.

6 Consequently, she is expected to be released from hospital later today.

7 Incredibly, the shop owners, who were sleeping upstairs, did not hear anything.

8 Understandably, the incident has unsettled local residents, many of whom have been victims of petty crime themselves in the past.

2 1 take part in f
2 worked together d
3 declined g
4 divided a
5 have come together b
6 make (it) possible h
7 approved c
8 annoy/anger e

3 Children's playground: encourage exercise, encourage outdoor play, increased social contact, positive for health
More bike lanes: encourage exercise, less pollution
More street seating: increased social contact, meeting places, positive for health, reduces fear of falling

4 Model answer
This essay looks at the question of what to do with old buildings that have lost their use, for example old churches that no one goes to or banks which have closed. There is a range of options, and to some extent the ideal solution will depend on the building in question, but two of the main possibilities are to demolish them or convert them into flats.

Looking at demolition first, it is easy to see that if buildings are demolished, the space they leave can be redeveloped into anything: an attractive square with a garden, where people can meet and enjoy local open space, or a new building for a new activity the area and community needs. With regards to the latter, this could be housing or a business use.

On the other hand, converting old buildings into flats is also an attractive proposition. Much of our history is contained in buildings and we can learn about our neighbourhood's past from learning about the former use of buildings. Furthermore, old buildings often have more character than new builds and create more attractive, people-friendly spaces. The downside is they are often expensive to refurbish and the layout of something like a church or office block may not be easily adapted into flats.

From my point of view, I think conserving old buildings is the most effective way of using public buildings, as long as the building itself is attractive. Old buildings embody the history of the area in contrast to new builds are often bland and characterless.

Get it right!
In some places it's happening more quickly and in some places more slowly.

Writing Part 2:1

1a Positive: absorbing, electric, emotionally charged, family-friendly, original, refreshing, riveting, talented, thought-provoking, touching
Negative: contrived, disjointed, implausible, mediocre, obvious, overrated, stereotypical, superficial, tasteless, unconvincing, wooden

1b Possible answers

An actor's performance	implausible, mediocre, overrated, stereotypical, talented, unconvincing, wooden
The development of the story or plot, treatment of the topic	absorbing, contrived, disjointed, electric, obvious, riveting
The concept/ approach	emotionally charged, family-friendly, highly original, refreshing, stereotypical, superficial, tasteless, thought-provoking

2a 1 in addition to
2 Besides
3 Not only
4 but
5 Moreover
6 Furthermore
7 What's more
8 along with

2b Likes: the clever interweaving of multiple stories, witty comments and sharp insights into the characters' actions and decisions, novel starts off well and has an initial buzz
Dislikes: new characters don't add anything special and are given too much importance, too many trivial anecdotes which distract

3 Model answer
There are so many great film moments. However, for me one of the best candidates for the Fantastic films website is the scene from *Singing in the Rain* where Gene Kelly sings the title song, 'Singing in the Rain'. I know lots of people think the scene final dance scene in *Dirty Dancing* where 'Johnny' played by Patrick Swayze and 'Baby' (Jennifer Grey) dance to 'The time of my life' is the most iconic dance scene of all time, but I disagree, and would go so far as to suggest it's not included.

In the *Singing in the Rain* scene, Don Lockwood played by Gene Kelly breaks into song to express his love for Kathy (Debbie Reynolds). He sings moving from pavement to a road full of puddles. Gene Kelly's dancing is fantastic and entertaining. The audience can also feel his happiness and can identify with his expression of newly found love.

In contrast, the dancing in *Dirty Dancing* while as technically accurate as Gene Kelly's lacks a sense of joy. In this scene, Johnny goes on stage to perform the last dance of the season at a holiday resort. He pulls 'Baby' on stage with him. The dance itself is nothing special by today's standards and not as entertaining. I would also argue that the whole film is not as good as *Singing in the Rain*, in terms of plot and entertainment value. The latter is clearly an all-time classic, while *Dirty Dancing* is just a typical film from the 1980s.

Writing Part 2:2

1 Positive aspects of the exhibition:
It exceeded expectations in terms of the number of people who attended.
The people who came had a passion for science.

What could be improved:
More hands on activities for children
Press and online publicity to attract a wider variety of visitors

2 Did the answer opposite:
1 make it clear who the report was for? ✓
2 use headings and clear layout? ✓
3 use a consistent and appropriate register and tone? ✓
4 use a range of language? ✓
5 explain the exhibition strengths and weaknesses? ✓
6 make recommendations for improvements? ✓

3a Words in the report are: *so, so as to, with a view to* and *in order to* were in the report.

3b 1 so as to
2 so/so that
3 in order not to/so as not to
4 so/so that
5 in order
6 With a view to
7 so as not to

4 Model answer
Introduction
The purpose of this report is to assess the science museum's suitability for school visits.
Findings
The science museum is one of the largest of its type in the country. It was recently renovated, and many new exhibits have been installed which make the visitors' experience a lot more 'hands on'. As a result, it is suitable for students with a range of learning styles.
Range of exhibits
The museum covers physics, biology (natural history) and chemistry. The physics exhibits are particularly interesting and clearly demonstrate the principles and laws students will have come across in lessons, such as Archimedes' principle and Newton's laws on gravity. The natural history part of the museum contains the oldest exhibits. Many of them, such as the dinosaur bones, still maintain a fascination for students, even if they don't necessarily correspond to today's curriculum.
In addition, there are many interesting exhibits on elements and chemical reactions.
Educational workshops
The museum has an educational department, which is happy to work with teachers to come up with worksheets and workshops specific to a school's needs. The worksheets are a very high standard and they mean that any visit can reinforce and clarify information learned in class.
Non-educational facilities
The museum has a room where students can eat their packed lunches and have pre- or post-visit talks and feedback. Furthermore, there is easy parking for coaches and wheelchair access for disabled students.
Conclusion
The museum provides an exceptional opportunity for students to have an enjoyable and educational school trip, because of the outstanding facilities on offer.

Writing Part 2:3

1 1 b/e   2 d/c   3 g   4 e/b
5 j   6 i   7 c   8 h
9 f   10 a
Formal: I hope to hear from you soon. Yours faithfully, Yours sincerely, I look forward to your reply.
Semi-formal: Kind regards. All the best, Looking forward to hearing from you.
Informal: Keep in touch! Best wishes, Write soon.

2 1 Question 1
2 Question 1 (asks for details of the branch where the writer works and the people who work there)
3 Useful language could be: *members of staff, colleagues, team*

3

a	*Dear Rodrigo,*	2
b	*Dear Ms Baker,*	1
a	*I am writing to give you information and my advice …*	1
b	*Thanks for your letter. Great news that …*	2
a	*(I'm, You'd, You'll …)*	2
b	no (*I am, You would, You will …)*	1
a	*What about … ? Try … Take it from me … I'd say that … You can take your pick …*	2
b	*I would highly recommend … You could try … Might I suggest … Another alternative might be …*	1
a	*would be ideal for you might (not) appeal would suit you best*	1
b	*your sort of thing you might fancy might tempt you*	2

4 Model answer

Dear Sir or Madam,

I am writing in response to your advert for teaching assistants for the International Summer Camp your company is organising this summer.

I am particularly interested in applying for a position as a Sports Teaching Assistant, although I would be willing to work on the crafts side too.

The reason why I think I would make a good member of your teaching team is that I am a member of several local sports clubs, including ones for swimming, athletics and badminton and regularly help with training sessions for new members. Furthermore, last summer, I went on a training course for badminton instructors and am now qualified to teach juniors and adults.

On the crafts side, I can paint in a variety of media and know how to weave, so I could help out with these activities if necessary.

In addition to my qualifications, I have been to several summer camps myself and know the problems young people face when they are away from home. I think this experience could prove invaluable, should I get the opportunity to work for you.

Ideally, I'd like to use my skills teaching swimming and badminton but, as I have a wide knowledge of sports, I could help out with any sport from athletics to zorbing. I have enclosed a cv with further details and hope you find my application interesting.

I look forward to hearing from you.

Yours faithfully,

Get it right!

My cousins and I used to collect all sorts of things.

Writing Part 2:4

1
1 overrun with tourists	5 uninterrupted views
2 on a shoestring	6 low-cost
3 at your leisure	7 off-the-beaten-track
4 low season	8 once-in-a-lifetime

2
1 In view of the fact that
2 For that reason/That is why
3 As a result
4 That is why/For that reason
5 Consequently/Therefore
6 Since
7 Thanks to
8 Therefore/Consequently

3 Model answer

To: Mr Brown, Head of History
Re: Proposed History Trip
<u>Introduction</u>
This is a proposal for a one-day history study trip in Liverpool.

<u>Options</u>
Looking at the options in the area, two attractions come to mind for an educational trip focusing on history: the Maritime Museum and Speke Hall.

The first option, the Maritime Museum tells the story of Liverpool as a port. It also documents world history through its focus on the growth of international trade (including the slave trade) and changes in maritime technology. It would be very easy to create worksheets for individual groups, who could then make presentations to the class in a subsequent lesson.

The museum is easily accessible by local buses.

The alternative, Speke Hall, provides a very well-preserved snapshot of what life was like in the 16th century. This would be a very useful trip for our students, as they study this period of history. Students would be able to study individual aspects of Tudor life (cooking, religion, transport) based on exhibits in the house. The Hall's education section also gives excellent talks.

Unfortunately, the house is only accessible by coach, which would add extra expense.

<u>Recommendation</u>
In my opinion, the most interesting option is the Maritime Museum. The exhibits have a clear focus, but at the same time cover in a lot of different aspects of history: social, economic and cultural. The Maritime Museum can also easily accommodate big groups of students and has better rates for groups, making it an ideal choice. It is also more easily accessible by local transport.

4 Students' own answers

Listening Part 1:1

1 1 B   2 C   3 C   4 A   5 B   6 C

Narrator:	**Track 1, Listening Part 1, Worksheet 1**
Narrator:	**You will hear three different extracts. For questions 1–6, choose the answer (A, B or C) which fits best according to what you hear. There are two questions for each extract.**
	Extract One. You hear two friends discussing the topic of reading books in printed or electronic form. Now look at questions one and two.
Woman:	What are you reading?
Man:	It's a novel … . quite gripping. Seeing me reading on my phone screen you'd never know what it was, would you? Anyway, it's nothing too cultured … It being electronic is a plus if you don't want people to see

easily what you're reading ... . I mean, if it isn't some great work of literature but something a bit trashy!

Woman: E-books have cured my terrible habit. I tend to skip bits. Especially if it's a thriller. I'll rush on, maybe 20 pages from where I am in the plot, just to give myself an idea of the ending. It can really spoil it though. But, I haven't figured out how to do it on this electronic reader.

Man: These electronic books sure beat carrying heavy books around, and if you decide you'd like a particular book you can just get it immediately, as long as you have a Wi-fi connection. Though, there's something about turning the pages and having a book in my hand that feels right.

Woman: And if you love a book, it stays on your shelf, like an old friend you can stop by and visit whenever you like.

Man: Of course e-books are always in your library too. They don't get battered like my most treasured paperbacks do.

Narrator: Now listen again.

Narrator: **Extract two. You hear a woman telling a friend about a book he gave her. Now look at questions three and four.**

Man: So, what did you think of the book I gave you?

Woman: *The Man in the Forest?* It was certainly an emotion-packed tale. There wasn't much about the man in the first half. I thought it got more gripping once he came into it more. I really identified with the main female character – the woman called Lucy. I can see why you thought it'd be my sort of thing – the blend of crime, mystery and social issues. It was quite disturbing in parts, as you suggested it would be. I did wonder why they chose that cover for the paperback edition though.

Man: What? The picture of the key? I thought it made the book look quite intriguing.

Woman: It doesn't really evoke the essence of what it's all about though. The book's chief strength is as a tightly plotted thriller that also draws attention to certain social injustices. I mean the image on the front cover has the potential to summarise the content or at least highlight the issues the book tackles, which it totally missed doing. If it had done, I'd have been more convinced it was going to be the kind of thing I'm typically drawn to. Still, it's sold over ten million copies, so what do I know ...

Narrator: Now listen again.

Narrator: **Extract three. You hear two writers talking about their daily routine. Now look at questions five and six.**

Man: My day starts with a look at the papers.

Woman: Oh, really? I deal with emails before anything else.

Man: Emails used to be exciting ... now it's all just stuff to clear. I'm pretty disciplined about checking them, but I find it doesn't hurt to switch off the internet most of the time ... although I sometimes need to consult it for reference. No, I start with the news and concentrate on the human-interest stories – I couldn't make up that kind of thing, so why bother, when I can get a spark of inspiration so easily ...

Woman: I've been meaning to tell you, I've started to write standing, with my keyboard and mouse at waist height. I reason that being on my feet for hours is a form of exercise. I think it wards off all those nasty things that start happening in the body when you're seated, though I'm probably kidding myself.

Man: Well, I force myself to take a long walk in the afternoon, but I wouldn't do it if I didn't have a voice in my head reminding me that it's also good for my brain. To be honest, I jump at the chance to opt out, say, if it's raining. If that's the case, I'll sometimes do some sit-ups indoors, but with a feeling of resignation.

Narrator: Now listen again.

2
1 declared	5 disclose
2 urge	6 reasoned
3 confided	7 speculating
4 grumbled	8 stipulates

3
1 to send Dee/that he would send Dee
2 wouldn't sell
3 is being made
4 he was finding writing
5 Anna (that) she
6 her daughter had had
7 reminded Ben to take / reminded Ben about taking / told Ben not to forget to take
8 to be
9 denied touching / denied having touched
10 agreed with Ruth

Listening Part 1:2
1 1 A 2 B 3 A 4 B 5 C 6 B

Narrator: Track 2. Listening Part 1, Worksheet 2	
Narrator: You will hear three different extracts. For questions 1–6, choose the answer (A, B or C) which fits best according to what you hear. There are two questions for each extract.	
Narrator: Extract one. You hear two friends talking about travelling on public transport. Now look at questions one and two.	
Man: I find commuter behaviour on public transport fascinating, especially at rush hour.	
Woman: Yeah, it's weird how uneasy it makes people being forced into such intimacy with strangers, all helplessly crowded in together. I guess that's why they read or listen to music and engage with fellow travellers so reluctantly … just to give up a seat for someone elderly or disabled and so on.	
Man: People approach each other so apologetically … mind you, half the time nobody registers that there's someone speaking to them because they're all wearing earplugs or headphones. And people put a bag on the seat next to them just to lower the chance of someone sitting there.	
Woman: Yet, apparently chatting and positive body language are actually more successful ways of getting to feel at ease than defensive strategies. I heard a radio programme about it. It seems the seat layout can be a problem: it's awkward to talk to anyone if you're right next to them, but if you're facing each other you can pick up key non-verbal signals which makes you feel less vulnerable. You'd think on regular commutes, where you often see the same faces in the same seats, it wouldn't be such a problem and people would be more at ease, but I'm not sure that's the case.	
Narrator: Now listen again.	
Narrator: Extract two. You hear two friends discussing the use of social media. Now look at questions three and four.	
Woman: I do sometimes wonder about the value of posting things on social media.	
Man: What do you mean?	
Woman: … so many people just give vent to anger or frustration. At any given moment, with all the different online platforms, there are thousands of people, who often don't know anything about the subject	

in question, telling others their ideas are rubbish. They should at least check their facts. I do. Anyway, I find it amazing when people react aggressively in public forums. I regularly post comments on various blogs, and pride myself on not over-reacting when someone has a go at something I've said, but it's hard not to. I do get angry too, but. I really don't …

Man: I guess there's something to be said for some sort of self-censoring rather than posting too wildly. The thing I find frustrating about social media is that it encourages an insatiable supply of short bits of infotainment – you know sharing news bites that are witty or shocking, and people tend not to think critically about what they read, but most of it's not even interesting, let alone true. I'm not including the kind of self-promotion a lot of people go in for on social media, photos of their wonderful holidays, or kids' graduation. That's all about wanting to look good to other people and mostly harmless.

Narrator: Now listen again.

Narrator: Extract three. You hear part of a radio programme in which two journalists are discussing surveys. Now look at questions five and six.

Man: There's so much we still have to learn about what influences human behaviour. We don't really know how to effect positive changes in what people do. Personally, I don't think our focus on large-scale surveys as the main source of insight into how people behave helps us. We hear all these sweeping statements about attitudes towards everything from brands to climate change, but the majority of research is built on self-reporting methodologies like surveys in which participants describe their own attitudes themselves. That's too narrow, because people's answers often depend on their mood or what's going on around them, or how they think they should answer, and that could certainly have implications when it comes to interpreting the results, especially if …

Woman: You mean they don't tell what causes people to change their behaviour?

Man: That's right.

Woman: There are actually some very interesting examples of companies adopting more unconventional strategies to finding ways to change behaviour. One soft drinks manufacturer recently launched a project with the aim of improving recycling behaviour. Rather than use the customary strategy of a huge consumer survey, the daily lifestyles of small samples of people were observed closely. Then they were invited to get involved in problem-solving processes. Of course, it may turn out to be ineffective, but I'd like to learn more about the research findings. It's all still ongoing.

Narrator: Now listen again.

2 1 affectionately
2 willingly
3 aggressively
4 Reluctantly
5 fearlessly
6 helplessly
7 nostalgically

3 1 Incorrect. The study said that most respondents believed that their driving skills were above average.
2 Correct
3 Correct
4 Incorrect. Richard told me that he was going to try to give up smoking before the course ended.
5 Correct
6 Incorrect. Liam said that he'd had stress-related nightmares in the previous month.

Listening Part 1:3

1 1 B 2 C 3 B 4 A 5 B 6 C

Narrator: 🔊 Track 3. Listening Part 1, Worksheet 3

Narrator: You will hear three different extracts. For questions 1–6, choose the answer (A, B or C) which fits best according to what you hear. There are two questions for each extract.

Narrator: Extract one. You hear two students talking about spending a gap year in Australia before going to university. Now look at questions one and two.

Woman: During my gap year in Australia, I met so many other Brits my age doing the same thing before going to uni back in the UK. They'd all done the same journey out there via Southeast Asia, stopping off briefly in Thailand and Bali on the way ... really unmissable places with jaw-dropping scenery ... .

Man: I made some good friends travelling in Australia in my gap year.

Woman: So often people claimed their main motivation for going was the unspoilt beaches, the wildlife, the rainforests – the endless sunshine. But that's true for lots of destinations. I actually think the major

additional lure is that there's one obstacle you don't have to overcome ... worrying about asking for directions or how to get around, which could be pretty daunting if you're staying somewhere for a while.

Man: It's a massive country – and surprisingly pricey. I took the bus between cities – flying really defeats the object of travel – so much of the country's character is revealed in those vast distances of pure nothingness. ... I did struggle to make ends meet. I earned a bit doing bits and pieces of work here and there. It wasn't easy to come by. Rather than pay high rent, I stayed in basic hostels. But it was good. I kept bumping into the same people, all on a tight budget of course.

Narrator: Now listen again.

Narrator: Extract two. You will hear two friends discussing the purpose of travelling. Now listen to questions three and four.

Woman: You're busy planning your next trip, Olly. Do you always feel a sense of purpose to your travels?

Man: To be honest, I might sometimes have felt like I've been there, done that, got the T-shirt. That's not often the case, but I do think you need to get off the beaten track. I try to go to new places. Once there, I'm a fan of just hanging out, and trying to get to understand the vibe of a place, and observe the way of life. I make a point of asking questions, so I can find places where I can chill out and discover what's going on ... rather than ticking it off as a place I've 'done' because I went on some amazing tour to a waterfall, or got a great picture of a tiger. You travel, what motivates you?

Woman: For me, it's about stepping out of my comfort zone – travelling alone gives you experiences that teach you about yourself. It's funny how what might have been a really bad experience, say, getting lost, or missing the only bus that day, can turn into an anecdote, which makes you see things differently. Having a story that ends up making your friends laugh, is quite cool really. Anyway, I've realised that although I'm pretty tough, tears come too easily when I'm tired and someone shouts at me.

Narrator: Now listen again.

Narrator: Extract three. You will hear two colleagues talking about a trip to a conference. Now listen to questions five and six.

Woman: So, flying to Edinburgh tomorrow for the conference. I can't wait.

Man:	Why so keen? We've both got to give talks tomorrow, that very afternoon.
Woman:	I know. I should really be looking at my presentation, and going over my latest improvements, so I remember them. I've been through it quite thoroughly, so I'm happy that the slides won't need to be altered.
Man:	You swore you'd listen to me go through mine one more time today.
Woman:	There's no cause to doubt my word!
Man:	You'd better not be joking about that!
Woman:	On condition you listen to my delivery too.
Man:	Sure. Anyway, I've no intention of making any major adjustments, I'd just appreciate some constructive criticism about whether I'm pausing in the right places, or speaking too fast, you know the sort of thing.
Woman:	Absolutely. That's what I need too. It'll be a relief not to be stuck in this cramped office. The renovations to our old one must have been going on for at least two months now. The prospect of getting away makes up for the weeks of preparation. Anyway, I've made a point of packing light so as not to have to drag a heavy case onto the airport train. I'd far rather have taken a taxi there … If only I'd been in charge of organising things!
Narrator:	Now listen again.

2 1 a 2 c 3 b 4 c 5 b 6 c

3 1 could have been
2 would have enjoyed
3 needn't be booked
4 would rather take
5 will leave

Get it right!
A time in history in which I would <u>have</u> liked to have been present is the Victorian era

Listening Part 2:1

1
1 necessary
2 achievement
3 chemistry
4 business
5 assistant
6 accommodation
7 beginning
8 measurement
9 research
10 psychologist

2
1 some   2 any   3 much
4 all   5 Both   6 no
7 such   8 a   9 certain
10 little

3
1 robots   2 garage   3 engine
4 toxic substances   5 software
6 (weather) balloon
7 ocean/ocean depths   8 attitude

Narrator:	Track 4. Listening Part 2, Worksheet 1
Narrator:	**You will hear a woman called Camilla Doyle introducing a science fair. For questions 1–8, complete the sentences with a word or short phrase.**

Welcome to this annual innovation fair, where we exhibit developments from the world of science. I'm Camilla Doyle, from the organising committee, and I'll take you through a few highlights, which I'm sure you're eager to learn more about.

If you've attended many science fairs before, you may be expecting to see such things as model volcanoes, crystals in jars, or robots. And it has to be said that a fair few robots have come under my scrutiny in my role on the selection committee over the years, but I'm certain everything you'll see today will give you cause for excitement.

So, what will you see? I'll start with an exhibit demonstrating an astounding feat by one young scientist, David Nelson, and his attempt to build a nuclear fusion reactor. One of the biggest challenges in physics is to create nuclear energy not by splitting atoms but fusing them together. David used the garage next to his house, rather than working in a science lab, to create a device that, though not self-sustaining, produces fusion on a tiny scale. Let's hope the neighbours don't complain of finding nuclear waste in his back garden!

If you're interested in motor racing, you'll be impressed by the achievements of a team who built a diesel-hybrid racing car that goes from nought to a hundred in just four seconds. They've developed a design that can also drive for 100 km using just 4.5 litres of petrol. The prototype for the engine is being refined, and they say their enhanced version will soon be ready.

Many industries are interested in Joe Higson's work. There are many types of chemicals, some more complex than others. Whichever they are, if used in the workplace, it's crucial to keep people safe, and Joe's machine helps with this. It sniffs out toxic substances in places they shouldn't be, a potential asset to any industry with regard to improving safety. I should say that Joe plans to adapt it for other purposes too.

The work of Jenny Benson is likely to yield huge dividends for space travel. It's crucial to use as little fuel as possible out in the depths of space, and there is a constant search for new types of energy. But efficiency is important too, and Jenny's ingenious software enables vehicles in space travel at accelerated speeds more economically, by navigating the obstacles in space more efficiently.

Some meteorology students have produced a balloon that's out of this world. They've created a camera-operated weather balloon and sent it over 30 km into the Earth's atmosphere. The readings they've got so far are incredibly detailed and could be helpful for weather forecasting and many other uses. The photographs taken by the balloon's camera are stunning too.

Something that's attracted media attention is another type of vehicle – an underwater rover that can operate in the harshest conditions. It can explore the ocean depths where there's absolutely no light, and it's being used to learn about the behaviour of the most difficult to reach marine life. There are hopes of taking it to the polar regions, where scientists hope to find out more about what might be living there.

It's been a privilege to chat to scientists exhibiting here. Their ambitions to find solutions to the problems on this planet are wonderful to see. The originality is extraordinary, though what shines through, above all, is their attitude. If something goes wrong, they work on it till they find an answer.

Narrator: Now listen again.

Listening Part 2:2

1 1 age
2 teamwork
3 string
4 a/one month
5 (travel) schedule
6 (in-country) partners
7 case studies
8 loneliness

Narrator: **Track 5. Listening Part 2, Worksheet 2**

Narrator: **You will hear a man called Sam Parker talking about doing volunteer work in other countries. For questions 1–8, complete the sentences with a word or short phrase.**

Woman: I'd like to tell you about some of the opportunities there are for international volunteering and a little about my own experiences. I should say, first of all, that most organisations prefer participants to

have qualifications or a particular skill. If you don't have these, it's crucial to consider what sort of impact you can have as a volunteer. It's also important to bear in mind that there are age requirements in certain countries.

My first volunteer experience was at a safari park in Thailand. It was rescue work taking care of birds that had been injured. Besides learning a lot about the bird's names and habits as well as all the various diseases they get, I also got to know more about wild cats, as there was a section of the park dedicated to them.

Teamwork's vital for all projects, and working on the project taught me an invaluable amount about this. I really developed my abilities in that respect. I guess it was the biggest takeaway thing for me.

Basically, when you volunteer you're there to get involved, and you'll have a lot of fun doing that. You might also pick up odd things like how to make a fire without matches, or how to build a hut with the most basic equipment. I'd built one before back home with my dad using screws and nails, so it was a real eye-opener for me when I was instructed in how to make one stay up using just string to keep it together. Volunteer work's as tiring as any job, but it can turn out to be a thoroughly enlightening experience.

With so many organisations offering volunteering placements abroad, it's not easy to determine which project might be the most ethical, sustainable, or beneficial. Generally speaking, the longer you stay the better. Short-term volunteering can be damaging to communities and it's generally advised that it's not appropriate to stay less than a month. It's often said that a commitment of around 12 weeks allows enough time for you to integrate with the local community and deliver useful work, so bear that in mind.

Your commitment also depends on what the organisation needs – it might need help delivering a specific project, such as reviewing the organisation's accounts or budgets, for example. Make sure you're working to their time frame, and not forcing them to adapt to your travel schedule.

Volunteer work abroad is sometimes offered by for-profit agencies based outside the country where the volunteer work takes place. They can allocate you to specific projects, or place you with a local organisation. If you use an agency, choose one that's transparent about its in-country partners and specifies which particular project you'll be working on.

Always ask questions about the impact of the volunteering programmes – the best ones will have strong case studies showing how well their projects are doing, which you can ask to look at prior to making any commitment. Look for projects that promote the positive integration of volunteers with the local community.

You'll usually have to pay a fee to volunteer, but food and accommodation are provided. I've volunteered all over the place, and in all my time, despite a few stomach aches and suffering from really bad flu once, the one thing that I'd fully expected to bother me didn't. That was loneliness. I always had people around who made it a truly amazing experience.

Narrator: Now listen again.

2a 1 a thoroughly/totally   b pretty/fairly
    c sort of/kind of
  2 a completely/absolutely b rather/somewhat
    c virtually/almost
  3 a slightly/a bit   b terribly/awfully
    c generally/mostly

2b 1 awfully   2 rather   3 kind of
  4 thoroughly 5 almost

3 1 unbelievably   6 unemployed
  2 loneliness   7 existence
  3 passionately   8 imperfect
  4 significance   9 disadvantaged
  5 noticeable

Listening Part 2:3

1 1 imagination   5 letters
  2 advertising agency 6 open spaces
  3 travel brochures   7 paper
  4 red hair   8 wisdom

Narrator: **Track 6. Listening Part 2, Worksheet 3**

Narrator: **You will hear a talk by a woman called Ellie Matthews about her life working as a writer and illustrator of children's books. For questions 1–8, complete the sentences with a word or short phrase.**

Woman: It's a pleasure to be here and tell you about my life as an illustrator and children's author ... a profession I really just fell into. It's not as if my art teacher or parents spotted any artistic skills in me when I was a young girl. They tended to focus on my vivid imagination ... I was always entertaining my friends with outrageous stories and so not really seen as a good influence at all!

However, I loved painting and opted to attend Art College. By graduation I'd accumulated a sizeable portfolio of work to showcase my talents and applied for jobs. I remember one was a position at a major art gallery; I didn't get it – fortunately as it turns out, but I felt crushed to be rejected for that and for a role at a big advertising agency. I do sometimes wonder how differently things might have panned out for me.

Anyway, I earned virtually nothing for two years, just bits and pieces doing illustrations for magazines and some work on a children's comic. The only financially rewarding thing I did in those early years as an illustrator was for travel brochures, but I wasn't enamoured by the idea of doing that forever.

Meanwhile, I'd been writing and drawing pictures for a children's book of my own about a girl called Carly. I sent the finished manuscript to various publishers and was stunned one day to hear that one of them wanted to publish it. To my amazement, the first edition of *Carly* flew off the shelves in bookshops. I think it was her red hair that made her such a distinctive character. She was a skinny little girl with super-thick glasses – somewhat based on my schoolgirl self. One source of inspiration for things she did and felt was going through letters written to my grandmother by my mum when I was young. They stirred my own vivid recollections ... like reading old diaries I guess, where the mention of some event or person triggers memories of a whole period of childhood.

Anyway, after *Carly*, I left Britain for the USA. I'd been taken there a lot as a child – my mother's parents lived there. I don't deal well with the cold in Britain, and I loved the friendliness over there. In addition, I've always adored its open spaces, and that's what influenced me to make the move to live and work there, rather than the weather. It's just so vast. I now share an apartment in New England with my husband and kids. In my studio

I have all the equipment I need. My drawing tools are pretty standard, though there are certain kinds of pens for fine lines I prefer and one specific brand of brush pens for more fluid lines. It's paper I'm terribly picky about. I can waste time with false starts if it isn't what I work best on. Marker pens, coloured pencils and inks are also essential tools of the trade.

Being a mother has changed me. I've had to learn patience. I've always been interested in the way children see things, and I love their funny expressions. I see every child as unique. That's the wisdom I've gained, and imparting it to my readers is a mission of mine. People believe children will bring them happiness, but it's more complex than that …

Narrator: Now listen again.

2 1 spent, was removed
    2 had been opened / was opened, became
    3 were living, were
    4 didn't/did not meet, were studying/studied/had been studying/had studied
    5 were spotted, had found

3a 1 draw attention   7 make a contribution
    2 cause concern   8 take exception
    3 make a move   9 draw support
    4 take heart   10 cause embarrassment
    5 draw a conclusion   11 make a point
    6 cause distress   12 take charge

3b 1 made a point
    2 to draw attention
    3 caused me embarrassment
    4 took heart

Get it right!

<u>A</u> <u>boat</u> <u>trip</u> <u>on</u> <u>the</u> <u>River</u> <u>Thames</u> <u>was</u> <u>planned</u> <u>for</u> <u>the</u> <u>next</u> <u>day</u>, but the weather was terrible and we couldn't go.

Listening Part 3:1

1 1 B 2 C 3 D 4 B 5 A 6 C

Narrator: **Track 7. Listening Part 3, Worksheet 1**

Narrator: **You will hear part of an interview with two graphic designers called Anita Dickinson and Joe Connolly in which they talk about going freelance. For questions 1–6, choose the answer (A, B, C or D) which fits best according to what you hear.**

Interviewer: With me on 'Work and Money' are two successful freelancers, Anita Dickinson

and Joe Connolly, who both worked as graphic designers at major companies but left to go it alone.

Woman: Hi.

Man: Hello.

Interviewer: Anita, tell us about your decision to go freelance.

Woman: Basically, I'd been working in a well-paid position for some time and I was undeniably proud of the fact that people at the company viewed the stuff I produced very favourably. No job's secure in today's economic climate, and I realised being employed wasn't necessarily as safe as I'd thought. I began a transition, doing freelance work on the side, and gradually building up a client base. My only doubt was whether this'd be enough to rely on to cover the salary and perks I'd lose by going it alone. Anyway, I've always been an independent person and the idea of being my own boss was ultimately irresistible.

Interviewer: What about you, Joe?

Man: One of the biggest excuses for not going freelance is not knowing how to get started. Clearly, you have to feel confident you know the craft, but beyond that, I simply exploited my own skills to the full and ensured I had a website that I thought would draw in clients. OK, so there was a little more to it than that, but getting started really wasn't all that complex, even if it took a while before business started pouring in. Fundamentally, it was about a willingness to sacrifice time, working evenings and weekends. Unfortunately, there's no room for any reluctance on that score. Being realistic about such things made it possible for me to become a full-time freelancer.

Interviewer: Do you enjoy working alone rather than with other people?

Man: Well, I thrived in the hustle and bustle of an office setting – working in teams, bouncing ideas off others, the odd joke with a colleague. I did seriously wonder if working alone would be my cup of tea. It can certainly lead to a sense of isolation for some. Whole days with just yourself for company might become unbearable. Fortunately for me, there are frequent opportunities for human contact – meetings, and consultations about certain contracts – almost too many. Thankfully, I've barely experienced any problems being on my own.

Interviewer: Is self-discipline very important, Anita?

Woman: As a freelancer, you're completely responsible for your own productivity.

	There's nobody there on a daily basis monitoring the amount you get done. I've experimented with some of the apps available for scheduling, or setting up reminders to keep you on track, but frankly, I find them unnecessary. I know I'm accountable solely to myself – and my clients, of course. If I didn't have that approach, I wouldn't have opted to work for myself. Frittering away time on social networks or browsing the web hardly occurs to me. I get so absorbed in my work that I'm more likely to end up working until late at night, which isn't great as you just end up utterly shattered the next day.
Man:	Yeah, and on top of all the day-to-day work you have to keep up with business trends.
Woman:	Mm … things move so fast, but I guess that keeping up is something non-freelancers have to do too.
Man:	If you're predominantly working in one specific area of the market, which tends to happen, then inevitably, you see how things are developing and adapt naturally.
Woman:	What's key is to have a niche and know it inside out. That way you're often ahead of others in the same game, saving you from constant time-consuming research into upcoming trends.
Man:	It's primarily a question of, as you say, being an expert, and having a real interest in what you're doing … in the end, easier than people think.
Woman:	And of course, as a designer, you always want to do the best work you can.
Interviewer:	You've both been very successful. Joe, what's the secret?
Man:	I've earned more being freelance than I ever could have with a company. Being competitive involves charging what I see as a sufficient return for the hours put in and considering what the client will regard as fair – that requires some bargaining. Sometimes, I've undersold myself, but it's worked in my favour. Because my work was high quality, word-of-mouth reports about this meant more work came my way. Arguing about whether what I'm charging is reasonable isn't a situation I've had to deal with.
Interviewer:	Well, thank you both very much indeed, and that's the end of the show today…
Narrator:	Now listen again.

2 1 admitted 2 confessed 3 recommend
      4 denied 5 insisted 6 suggested
      7 oppose 8 claims

3 1 g (A large investment inevitably involves some risk)
      2 a
      3 d
      4 e (In its first year the company barely made any money but things went improved later.)
      5 h (Joe works from home a lot of the time.)
      6 c
      7 f
      8 b (Shareholders are always interested in getting a good return on their investment.)

Listening Part 3:2

1 1 B   2 C   3 D   4 A   5 B   6 D

Narrator:	🔊 Track 8. Listening Part 3, Worksheet 2
Narrator:	**You will hear an interview in which two people called Claire MacBride and Shaun Kale are talking about training to run in a charity marathon. For questions 1–6, choose the answer (A, B, C or D) which fits best according to what you hear.**
Interviewer:	Today, I'm interviewing Claire MacBride and Shaun Kale, who both recently ran a marathon for the first time. Claire, what made you train for the marathon?
Woman:	I decided to have a stab at it as a way of raising money for charity. I wasn't the sporty type who typically runs distances of 42 kilometres! The very idea made me shudder. When I've heard people making resolutions to turn over a new leaf at new year, I've always been sceptical, so I assumed my resolve would wear off once I began training. I can't quite work out how I became that annoying person who'd arrive at work glowing with satisfaction at having run ten kilometres to work. I relished those runs and when I got into conversations with colleagues about nightmare commutes, I'd shrug my shoulders and say: "I'm so glad I run to work!"
Interviewer:	Shaun, how was your marathon preparation? Did things go right for you?
Man:	Well, I'd always been an enthusiastic athlete and believed anyone with grit and enough preparation could do the marathon, but it was obvious I needed to have a clearly thought out training strategy. I already had a fair base fitness level, so I set out to bank some big distances early on. But I became conscious I'd underestimated the mental struggle. I'd failed to grasp how critical it was to find ways to spur myself on – to

reach the number of kilometres that go into building up the necessary endurance without giving up. If I'd factored in ways to get over my resistance in the early stages, I'd have tackled the challenge more effectively.

Interviewer: Isn't injury a risk during marathon training?

Woman: Absolutely. One day, I suddenly developed excruciating pains in my right thigh, so bad that abandoning the whole thing may have crossed my mind briefly. However, I headed off to a physio trainer who told me to take it easy for a week and refrain from running, and to do just light swimming. I was reluctant to disrupt the routine I'd got into, so I just carried on anyway ... then fell ill with bronchitis. The hardest thing about marathon training is knowing how not to overdo it. Anyway, I was forced to rip up my schedule and set myself one based on being more in tune with my physical self.

Interviewer: How did it feel getting up to train on winter mornings?

Woman: Friends told me 'It'll be so lonely and miserable'. I know there are visualisation techniques to conquer negative feelings, you picture yourself racing along ahead of the pack, any image that'll induce you to get up and out. But then you confront the reality of heading out through the park in the darkness of a January dawn: there's hardly another runner to be seen. It's amazing what you find to focus on: the cooing of pigeons, the rustling of leaves, the crunch of trainers on gravel. Focussing on insignificant things enabled me to endure the monotony and the icy winds.

Interviewer: Was your running speed in the marathon a concern, Shaun?

Man: During my training I tried some half-marathons. Using my time for them, I tried to calculate my speed across the full distance using software. Of course, it's double the distance, stamina, everything, but the claim is that your performance on the marathon can be predicted based on other times and distances you've run, assuming you make it to the end. Obviously, the fitter you are the more you can hold on to your pace for longer. Using apps got me into the whole process of establishing targets. Within any gadget-based prediction there's leeway of course. It couldn't take into account anything that happened on race day, or how I'd trained.

Interviewer: So, how was the experience on the day?

Man: Running a marathon's a huge undertaking. Uplifting isn't the word. The weather was dreadful, but a massive crowd turned out, and the applause ringing out on all sides was overwhelming. But there was also the hassle of locating my loyal friends and family. Despite agreeing a spot at the end of the route, exasperatingly, when I passed the finish line they were nowhere to be seen among the endless spectators.

Woman: For me, it took time to sink in that I'd made it. During the race I wondered if my body might let me down, my legs were like lead, and before the finish I tumbled, which wasn't how I'd envisioned things. Somehow, I dragged myself up and staggered over the line, only to collapse in a heap, oblivious to the cheering and clapping. I gather people came to my rescue. I don't think anyone who hasn't tried it can fully appreciate what it feels like to achieve a goal like that.

Interviewer: Well, congratulations ...

Narrator: Now listen again.

2a 1 d 2 a 3 f 4 e 5 c 6 g 7 b

2b
1 spur on
2 wore off/had worn off
3 is factored in
4 build up
5 let himself in for
6 refrain from
7 turned out

3
1 'd/had factored, 'd/would have tackled
2 'd/would have scored, 'd/had had
3 wouldn't/would not have tried, hadn't/had not spent
4 hadn't/had not eaten, wouldn't/would not have ended
5 'd have had/would have had, hadn't/had not been
6 'd/would have been, hadn't/had not been

Listening Part 3:3

1 1 C 2 C 3 A 4 D 5 B 6 D

Narrator: Track 9. Listening Part 3, Worksheet 3

Narrator: You will hear two students called Jolie and Alan talking about a TV series they watch called 'The Sensing Brain'. For questions 1–6, choose the answer (A, B, C or D) which fits best according to what you hear.

Woman: So, Alan, did you see the latest episode of 'The Sensing Brain'?

Man: Yes, Jolie, it was interesting.

Woman:	So, I gather from the reviews. I missed it, so you can tell me about it ... though I'll probably watch it online.
Man:	There was this woman who's an expert on perfume making and runs workshops on the subject. It seems humans can improve their sense of smell fairly rapidly with practice. Even those who are convinced they've got a terrible one can prove pretty adept if they apply themselves.
Woman:	I wonder if it's like music. If you haven't studied or listened to a lot, you're hard-pushed to spot the difference between a clarinet and an oboe, but once you've put in some time you can distinguish them effortlessly.
Man:	Apparently so – even if you haven't done specialist training. I learnt a bit about perfumes actually. There's an amazing range of terms to classify them.
Woman:	I guess most of us have a restricted vocabulary and struggle to describe scents. Whereas experts have been trained to recognise and name subtle nuances that pass the average person by. I remember trying to describe this white musk perfume I liked to a woman in a perfume shop and I was saying I wanted something dark, deep and heavy, but she actually saw the perfume I was after as light, sweet and fluffy. I'd imagined the word musk described the exact opposite.
Man:	According to the programme, one thing people tend to feel pretty certain about is their ability to spot the difference between a natural and synthetic aroma.
Woman:	Yeah, synthetic smells are so fake.
Man:	Well, they've done tests, and take for example, lime essential oil which is sharply intense. The vast majority of subjects in the lab actually identify it as smelling chemical, while the artificial odour lime oxide is seen as smooth and natural. And there's this chemical that has an almond-like smell, and it's universally seen as natural, apart from by chemists and chefs.
Woman:	How interesting. So, was the programme all about smell then?
Man:	It was a big focus. It also dealt with human and animal brains. Way back, there was this scientist who found that the brain region in humans that processes odour detection is smaller, relative to total brain volume, than in dogs or rats. New findings show the number of neurons, you know nerve cells in the brain, related to smell is remarkably consistent across mammals.
	Of course, you have to be careful of what you read into measurements and how they're used. Mice have more genes for smelling than humans, so that's seen as a sign of their superiority, but it may be that there isn't a tight relationship between genes and ability.
Woman:	There are likely to be new studies in the future that tell us more. The review I read said there was some stuff about music and the brain.
Man:	Yeah, about our ability to pay attention to working or studying while listening to music. Personally, if I'm trying to study, music either takes me over emotionally or I start to analyse it.
Woman:	True. I like music too much not to pay attention to it, whatever its quality and whatever I'm doing, unfortunately! But there *are* those who find it impossible to work without playing music.
Man:	Different strokes for different folks. I know a classically-trained musician who just can't work without headphones on.
Woman:	Music's a language, and it's virtually impossible to concentrate on two at the same time without losing details of one or both. If we all went back to paying attention to one thing at a time, our awareness would be much deeper, music included.
Man:	Some people claim the internet's changing how our brains work.
Woman:	That's what the next episode's about! With a focus on the human brain in response to new technology. It's essential to be conscious of the fact that we're used to dealing with a constant stream of information. After all, that's what the real world is, as far as our senses are concerned, either staring at a tennis video game or actually on the court playing, the brain does the same amount of work. Both activities are providing detailed sensory information. Fortunately, the brain doesn't bother to process absolutely everything that comes in, it filters things out, and uses a sort of 'best guess' of what's important. It's already well adapted to prevent information overload, so it's unlikely the internet would cause such a thing.
Man:	I do feel panicked by the amount of information out there sometimes. Always running just to stand still.
Woman:	Well, there's a lot more to learn out there ...
Narrator:	Now listen again.

Get it right!

You can find out everything you want if <u>you</u> <u>just</u> press the button.

2
1 either	2 so	3 ours
4 those	5 one	6 ones
7 such	8 neither	9 not

3
1 is almost certainly going to specialise
2 is more than likely to be
3 looks increasingly probable that
4 are not absolutely sure that
5 are far more likely to suffer
6 in the unlikely event of
7 there will undoubtedly be
8 seems highly improbable to me that / seems to me highly improbable that

Listening Part 4:1

1 1 G 2 B 3 C 4 H 5 E 6 F 7 H 8 B
9 A 10 E

Narrator: 🔊 **Track 10. Listening Part 4, Worksheet 1**

Narrator: **You will hear five short extracts in which people are talking about the environment. For questions 1–5, choose from the list (A–H) what each speaker enjoys about what they do to look after the environment.**

For questions 6–10, choose from the list (A–H) how each speaker feels about global environmental issues.

Speaker 1: Politicians really could do a lot more about the waste of resources. But it's also up to individuals to do their bit. It causes me great annoyance that I'm unable to change things on a large-scale – there's so much unnecessary rubbish building up everywhere. Anyway, I decided to enquire into joining a local environmental group involved in doing things on a minor level. Although people in the group argue about how to tackle the problem, we do our best to get things recycled that might otherwise end up in the sea or strewn around the countryside. It's a source of pleasure to have a regular activity on a weekly basis that's aimed at actually trying to do something.

Speaker 2: One thing that can help the environment is to eat less meat – so many of the world's resources go into producing it – and it's very heartening to hear of the number of people switching to vegetarian and vegan diets. It's a sign that change is on the way and people are waking up to the need to take care of our planet. I was strongly advised against going vegan by some people who said it was a big mistake, and food would cost more, but that doesn't seem to be true. Actually, it's been fantastic how friends have taken the trouble to make special meals for me, though I still miss meat sometimes.

Speaker 3: I honestly believe we have a real hope of saving our environment. Most people I know find it rewarding, as I do myself, to feel that they aren't doing some of things that are terrible for the environment like flying and driving excessively, but it is up to the authorities to adopt the right course of action. If governments implement what they talk about, then real change is possible. I'm inclined to think that progress is starting in that respect after some mistaken strategies. Big businesses also have a lot of power, and so do journalists who write about climate change and influence the public debate.

Speaker 4: Fossil fuels damage the environment, and it's not at all clear what the best strategy to deal with the problem is. I've heard that nuclear energy has some benefits as well as drawbacks. It's easier said than done to solve the environmental problems we all face, and I haven't got any real answers. But I'm still confident that the experts are working hard to find a solution. I try to take on board what I hear about in the press and on TV, and I don't mind spending money on good books about the environment that'll help me get to grips with the facts. I find it satisfying to try and understand the complexity of the issues.

Speaker 5: Some people make a big thing about the importance of recycling, and that kind of thing, but what they don't take into account, and it's something I worry about, is how effective that kind of action really is. It's expensive and uses energy just collecting and processing all the material. I do get a buzz though out of convincing friends to reduce their energy use – by doing the sort of things I do, like turning down the heating, investing in insulation, or cycling instead of driving. It's about *reducing* the world's carbon emissions and some people in the media are pushing this idea – it'd be a serious error not to listen to them.

Narrator: Now listen again.

---

2 1 b 2 c 3 a 4 c 5 c 6 a 7 b 8 a

3 1 line   2 drive   3 board   4 go
   5 wake   6 bit   7 respect   8 said
   9 grips   10 trouble

Listening Part 4:2

1 1 G 2 B 3 D 4 F 5 H 6 G 7 F 8 H
   9 A 10 C

Narrator: 🔊 Track 11. Listening Part 4, Worksheet 2

Narrator: **You will hear five short extracts in which people are talking about working as actors. For questions 1–5, choose from the list (A–H) what has helped the speaker to succeed.**
For questions 6–10, choose from the list (A–H) what each speaker regrets about the past.

Speaker 1: I've always been a conscientious person. I trained in music and it was my talent for singing that drew me into the theatre. I started to act in plays with roles that involved singing, loved the acting side and went on train to be an actor. It took a lot of persistence to get the parts I get. There were lots of setbacks, but I hung on and just kept at it. It's taken time but now I'm never short of work. I was always determined to get better parts than anyone else when I was younger, which is something I feel uncomfortable thinking about now. I was very single-minded you might say.

Speaker 2: This career's all about doing new things and meeting new people. I had so much fun training to be an actor … that's not to say I wasn't fully committed to my studies. I was. It's been a struggle getting to where I am today. I was devastated when a film I almost appeared in won dozens of awards. I completely misjudged the script when I said no to a major part. If only I could rewrite history. That was a bit of a one-off as normally I'm only too happy not to play it safe. I thrive on working in drama that pushes the boundaries and challenges accepted norms… that's probably my biggest asset actually.

Speaker 3: As an actor I've always preferred the theatre to film. I love the buzz of an audience. I really should have made more of my music and drama degree, but I got in with a crowd of mates and we… let's say… lived life to the full, you know, staying up all night and stuff. It's not that we didn't want to do well, just we were over-confident I guess. Anyway, I'm lucky enough to have performed with some great people – especially in comedy. Directors seem to spot how outgoing I am – I'll do pretty much anything, and not get hung up about looking silly. That quality of mine has served me pretty well actually.

Speaker 4: I'd always enjoyed acting and drama, so it was a mystery to everyone when I opted to do a law degree. I put everything I had into it but soon realised I'd never make it to the end of the course. It wasn't me, and it took me a while to realise that. I've been told I've got a magnetic personality and maybe that's why this friend's dad who was a director wanted me for a part in his film. Anyway, the film won an award, and I haven't looked back … offers of work keep rolling in. I haven't had to be ruthless to get where I am fortunately. Competing against others is something I detest.

Speaker 5: I'm quite a shy person, but in fact my cool exterior is deceptive. I'm pretty intense about my work. I knew from the beginning I'd go on the stage, and I threw myself into my degree in performing arts. The role that first got me noticed was in a soap opera. I wish I'd been a bit more accepting of colleagues in the early days though. Nothing anyone did seemed good enough. I was such a perfectionist. My devotion to developing what I do feels like a never-ending process, but it's what got me where I am today. I want to do more musicals, so I'm working on my singing voice at the moment.

Narrator: Now listen again.

---

2 1 c 2 e 3 b 4 d 5 a 6 h 7 i 8 f 9 g

3 1 hadn't/had not wasted
   2 had had
   3 could sing
   4 turning down/having turned down
   5 have been
   6 hadn't chosen
   7 not trying/not having tried
   8 would/could/might have turned out

Listening Part 4:3

1 1 H 2 A 3 G 4 D 5 F 6 F 7 H 8 C
   9 E 10 B

Narrator: 🔊 Track 12. Listening Part 4, Worksheet 3

Narrator: You will hear five short extracts in which people are talking about taking part in a public event. For questions 1–5, choose from the list (A–H) what each speaker feels about what they are doing.

For questions 6–10, choose from the list (A–H) each speaker's main reason for taking part.

Speaker 1 Running a half-marathon wasn't something I ever really expected to find myself doing. It's to raise money to support an organisation that campaigns about homelessness. The thing that drives me to do things like this is a desire to explore the various ways of bringing about change and see which has the most impact. I find it appalling that there are people without somewhere to live through no fault of their own. If the media were to draw more attention to the subject I might not feel I've got to do things like this. It'll be the first of many runs until there's a situation where more public money goes into dealing with the problem.

Speaker 2: I'm entering an article about genetic engineering into a science writing competition run by a national newspaper, and I'll be competing against some excellent writers. Fortunately, I haven't had to make huge financial sacrifices – you know unpaid time doing research. I was pleased about that. I was able to write knowledgeably as the subject's something I knew a lot about from my studies. I did have to simplify things for a popular audience though. Even if I don't win, I'll have achieved what I set out to do as long as I make some useful contacts. I'll be at the results ceremony and intend to socialise since science journalism is the area I intend to make my name in.

Speaker 3: One thing I've often observed in myself is a reluctance to be the centre of attention. I don't seek out the limelight, but when the leader of the orchestra I play with asked me to play a solo part in a performance I said OK. I felt it would make me focus on developing my talents instead of just taking a back seat. I don't want to throw away all the energy, hours and effort I've put into becoming a skilled musician. People have been so supportive and given me lots of tips that were extremely welcome. If I were to mess things up, I guess there's always a next time, but I'm hoping that won't be the case.

Speaker 4: People who know me were quite surprised to hear I was going to give a public talk. It's at an event about building design and my aim is to make it clear that a lot can be done at the local level to try and limit the number of tall buildings. It's something I feel strongly about, and I've spent a lot of time working on what I'm going to say. I'm pretty sure everything'll go according to plan. I've rehearsed it enough times. I'm covering aspects of the issue that I think are relevant to local people and I intend to convince them that doing something constructive is easier than they think.

Speaker 5: I'm helping organise a free concert in my area. It's not a massive event but I've never done anything like this, so I'm looking forward to it being over and done with actually. The pressure's quite intense because of the planning involved. I really believe in encouraging young musicians to get out there and show off their skills. We've got funding for the concert from some big companies and it was me who drafted the report to demonstrate what they'd gain from investing. That's something that motivated me to get involved as knowing how to do things like that effectively should ensure I have the kind of expertise that'll improve my career prospects.

Narrator: Now listen again.

Get it right!

Employers won't accept those excuses, and to be honest I won't <u>either</u>.

2
1. simplifying
2. demonstrating
3. socialising
4. seeking out
5. observing
6. campaigning
7. covering
8. drafting

3
1. is done
2. to draw
3. aren't/are not
4. don't/do not talk
5. have
6. hadn't/had not been
7. to be avoided
8. doesn't/does not try

Speaking Part 1:1

1a
1. opportunities
2. chances
3. possibility
4. prospect
5. particular
6. important
7. significant
8. unique

1b Students' own answers

2a 1 d 2 b 3 a 4 f 5 e 6 c

Narrator: 🔊 **Track 13 Speaking Part 1, Worksheet 1 Exercise 2a**

Examiner: Good morning. My name is Julie Grimes and this is my colleague Sam Johnson. And your names are?

Kriska: Kriska Varga.

Franz: Franz Schuler.

Examiner: Can I have your mark sheets, please? Thank you.
First of all, we'd like to know something about you.
Where are you from, Kriska?

Kriska: I'm from Hungary.

Examiner: And you, Franz?

Franz: I'm from Austria.

Examiner: Kriska, what is your favourite free-time activity at the moment?

Kriska: Currently, I prefer to do outdoor activities, like hiking or jogging. I try and keep myself fit. Sometimes I go alone and other times with friends.

Examiner: Franz, what sort of work would you most like to do in the future?

Franz: Well, I'm studying economics, so I guess I'd prefer something related to finance. Perhaps banking or accounting.

Examiner: Kriska, if you had the opportunity, would you take a year out and travel?

Kriska: That would be fantastic! Of course, I'd need to save up beforehand. And maybe I'd need to do some work to survive financially. As I love discovering new places, it would be right up my street!

Examiner: Franz, what sort of things do enjoy learning?

Franz: When studying, I generally prefer figures to letters, but I do enjoy a good history book. And I find documentaries intriguing.

Examiner: Kriska, do you like to give yourself aims and targets?

Kriska: It depends. I have work ambitions, but outside work I like to take each day as it comes.

Examiner: Franz, are you planning to do any courses in the near future?

Franz: Right now, I'm just hoping to pass this exam! Once I've finished, I suppose I might take up another language. I quite fancy that.

2b Students' own answers

3a 1 What free-time activity do you enjoy most?
2 What sort of work would you like to do in the future?

3 If you had the opportunity would you take a year out to travel?
4 What sort of things do you enjoy learning?
5 What would your ideal job be?
6 Are you planning to do any courses in the near future?
7 How easy is it for you to meet new people where you live?
8 How do you find out about things that interest you?

Narrator: 🔊 **Track 14 Speaking Part 1, Worksheet 1 Exercise 3a**

Examiner: 1 What free-time activity do you enjoy most?
2 What sort of work would you like to do in the future?
3 If you had the opportunity would you take a year out to travel?
4 What sort of things do you enjoy learning?
5 What would your ideal job be?
6 Are you planning to do any courses in the near future?
7 How easy is it for you to meet new people where you live?
8 How do you find out about things that interest you?

3b Students' own answers

Speaking Part 1:2

1 1 d 2 g 3 a 4 c 5 e 6 b 7 h 8 f

2 1 is
2 kicks
3 like
4 you'll love
5 will be broadcast
6 we'll be showing
7 will continue
8 will have been watching
9 are

3a See audio

Narrator: 🔊 **Track 15 Speaking Part 1, Worksheet 2, Exercise 3a**

Examiner: Good morning. My name is Karen Smith and this is my colleague Jamie Dathorne. And your names are?

Jae: Jae Young.

Mario: Mario Gimelli.

Examiner: Can I have your mark sheets, please? Thank you.
First of all, we'd like to know something about you.
Where are you from, Jae Young?

Jae: I'm from Korea.

Examiner: And you, Mario?

Mario: I'm from Italy.

Examiner: 1 What do you think you will be doing in five year's time?

2 Which teacher will you always remember?

3 What are you going to watch on TV this week?

4 What do you hope to have achieved by the time you're 60?

5 Have you seen anything interesting at the cinema recently?

6 How important is it to have friends who share the same interests as you?

7 What is the best time of year to visit your country?

8 Do you find it easy to relax?

3b Students' own answers

Speaking Part 1:3

1 1 journey
2 tour
3 visits/excursions
4 excursions/visits
5 trip
6 voyage
7 travels

2 1 made
2 travel
3 catch/take
4 went
5 take/use
6 do/cover
7 done
8 spend

Get it right!

In front of the metro station there's a taxi rank, where <u>you will probably</u> find a taxi waiting.

3 Possible answers

1 will certainly/most definitely/undoubtedly

2 may/might/could possibly

3 probably won't/will probably/may/might possibly

4 may possibly/ probably won't

5 certainly won't/could possibly

6 will certainly

7 will probably not

4a 1 celebrate
2 concerned
3 important
4 wish
5 change
6 won
7 meet
8 affect

Narrator: 🔊 **Track 16 Speaking Part 1, Worksheet 3, Exercise 4a**

Examiner: Good morning. My name is James Wilson and this is my colleague Amanda Putney. And your names are?

Kai: Kai Sakamoto

Sandrine: Sandrine Thirion.

Examiner: Can I have your mark sheets, please? Thank you.
First of all, we'd like to know something about you.
Where are you from, Sandrine?

Sandrine: I'm from Belgium.

Examiner: And you, Kai?

Kai: I'm from Japan.

Examiner: 1 How do you think you might celebrate your next birthday?

2 Do you think we should live for today or not be concerned about tomorrow?

3 How important is being adventurous to you?

4 Which places are on your wish list?

5 If you could change one thing about the area you live, what would it be?

6 What would you do if you suddenly won a lot of money?

7 Which famous person would you like to meet?

8 If you were without the internet for a week, how would it affect you?

4b Students' own answers

Speaking Part 2:1

1a 1 cross-country
2 cutting-edge
3 last-minute
4 long-term
5 record-breaking
6 time-consuming

1b 1 record-breaking
2 Cross-country
3 cutting-edge
4 Long-term
5 time consuming
6 last-minute

2 1 the ~~more~~ **most** suitable
2 ~~most~~ clear**est**
3 big**g**est challenge
4 much ~~more~~ lower and ~~slowlier~~ slower than
5 ~~most~~ favourite
6 ~~bests~~ best

3 Students' own answers

Narrator: 🔊 **Track 17 Speaking Part 2 Worksheet 1 Exercise 3**

Examiner: In this part of the test, I'm going to give each of you three pictures. I'd like you talk about two of them on your own for about a minute, and also to answer a question briefly about your partner's pictures.
Sara, It's your turn first. Here are your pictures. They show people doing different physical activities.
I'd like you to compare two of the pictures and say how difficult it might be for the people to do these different activities and what benefits the people might get from doing these activities in groups.
All right?

Examiner: Thank you.

Juan, which activity do you think would be the most enjoyable for the people involved?

Examiner: Thank you. Can I have the booklet, please? Now, Juan, here are your pictures. They show people attending different events.

I'd like you to compare two of the pictures, and say why the people might enjoy going to these events and how difficult the events might be to organise.

All right?

Examiner: Thank you. Sara, which of these events do you think would attract the largest crowd?

Examiner: Thank you. Can I have the booklet, please?

Speaking Part 2:2

1 1 a great deal
2 more extraordinary
3 as far back as
4 more and more
5 more straightforward
6 much more thoughtful
7 less spontaneous

2 1 have left
2 keep
3 forward
4 verify
5 comes, raising
6 printing, storing

Narrator: 🔊 **Track 18 Speaking Part 2 Worksheet 2 Exercise 3**

Examiner: In this part of the test, I'm going to give each of you three pictures. I'd like you to talk about two of them on your own for about a minute, and also to answer a question briefly about your partner's pictures.

Natalia, it's your turn first. Here are your pictures. They show people doing things together. I'd like you to compare two of the pictures and say why the people might have chosen to do these things together and how the people might be feeling.

All right?

Examiner: Thank you.

Vlad, which activity do you think needed the longest preparation?

Examiner: Thank you. Can I have the booklet, please? Now, Vlad, here are your pictures. They show people making decisions in different situations.

I'd like you to compare two of the pictures, and say why the people might be making these decisions and how difficult it might be to make the decisions. All right?

Examiner: Thank you. Natalia, which decision do you think needs the most careful consideration?

Examiner: Thank you. Can I have the booklet, please?

Speaking Part 2:3

1 1 may/might have been
2 can
3 may/might
4 must be
5 might/may have been
6 might not have
7 can
8 may not
9 can
10 might/can
11 can/might
12 could have been

2 Students' own answers

Get it right!
'Do you see the baby foxes?' I asked. Thomas was very excited and he said, 'Yes, I see. But their mother must be there somewhere too.'

Narrator: 🔊 **Track 19 Speaking Part 2 Worksheet 3 Exercise 3**

Examiner: In this part of the test, I'm going to give each of you three pictures. I'd like you talk about two of them on your own for about a minute, and also to answer a question briefly about your partner's pictures.

Su Ling, it's your turn first. Here are your pictures. They show people making things. I'd like you to compare two of the pictures and say why the people might be making these things and what problems they might have.

All right?

Examiner: Thank you.

Anuman, which of these things might take the longest to make?

Examiner: Thank you. Can I have the booklet, please? Now, Anuman, here are your pictures. They show people restoring things. I'd like you to compare two of the pictures, and say why the people might be restoring these things and how patient they might need to be.

All right?

Examiner: Thank you. Su Ling, which of these things might be the most difficult to restore?

Examiner: Thank you. Can I have the booklet, please?

Speaking Parts 3&4:1

1 1 therapy
2 sympathetic
3 obsession
4 fear
5 upset
6 insecurity
7 reaction
8 phobia

2 Students' own answers

3 Students' own answers

> **Narrator:** **Track 20 Speaking Parts 3&4 Worksheet 1 Part 3 Exercise 3a**
>
> **Examiner:** Now, I'd like you to talk about something together for about two minutes. Here are some things that can affect our mood and a question for you to discuss. First you have some time to look at the task.
> Now, talk to each other about how these different things can affect our mood.
>
> **Examiner:** Thank you. Now you have about a minute to decide which of these things you think most affects people's moods.

4 Students' own answers

> **Narrator:** **Track 21 Speaking Parts 3&4 Worksheet 1 Part 4 Exercise 3b**
>
> **Examiner:** Do you think it's better to show your feelings or to hide them?
> Would you say that you are generally in a good mood or a bad mood?
> Some people say that laughter is a good form of therapy. What do you think?
> Do you think that young people today suffer more from stress at school than they used to?
> Do you think people become less tolerant as they grow older?
> Do you believe that children should be taught to manage their feelings at school?
> Thank you. That is the end of the test.

Speaking Parts 3&4:2

1 1 You may well be right.
2 The best solution could be for rubbish to be collected more frequently.
3 I would just like to suggest an alternative.
4 It's sort of difficult to choose.
5 I wonder if you could give more details.
6 I tend to agree.
7 That is not necessarily the case.
8 It may be argued that temperatures are rising.

2a 1 fair   6 disagree
2 totally   7 wouldn't
3 see   8 way
4 more   9 look
5 sure   10 far

2b Students' own answers

3 Students' own answers

> **Narrator:** **Track 22 Speaking Parts 3&4 Worksheet 2 Part 3 Exercise 3a**
>
> **Examiner:** Now, I'd like you to talk about something together for about two minutes. Here are some things that we can do to help the environment and a question for you to discuss. First you have some time to look at the task.
> Now, talk to each other about how useful these actions are in helping the environment.
>
> **Examiner:** Thank you. Now you have about a minute to decide which of these actions you think is the most important to do.

4 Students' own answers

> **Narrator:** **Track 23 Speaking Parts 3&4 Worksheet 2 Part 4 Exercise 3b**
>
> **Examiner:** Do you think it would be a good idea to reward people who help the environment and punish those who don't?
> Do you think you personally do enough to help save our planet?
> At what age do you think children should be made aware of environmental problems?
> Do you think governments can cooperate to help the environment?
> What part can the media play in encouraging people to help the environment?
> Are you optimistic or pessimistic about the future of the planet?
> Thank you. That is the end of the test.

Speaking Parts 3&4:3

1a 1 d   2 f   3 a   4 b
5 c   6 g   7 e

1b Students' own answers

Get it right!
We want to build a school and a playground. <u>In addition</u>, we want to build shops near the new houses.

2 Students' own answers

3 Students' own answers

> **Narrator:** **Track 24 Speaking Parts 3&4 Worksheet 3 Part 3 Exercise 3a**
>
> **Examiner:** Now, I'd like you to talk about something together for about two minutes.
> Here are some skills that people think are important for their working lives today and

	a question for you to discuss. First you have some time to look at the task.
Examiner:	Now, talk to each other about how important these skills are for people's working lives today and why.
Examiner:	Thank you. Now you have about a minute to decide which of these skills you think will be most important to have in the future.

4 Students' own answers

Narrator:	Track 25 Speaking Parts 3&4 Worksheet 3 Part 4 Exercise 3b
Examiner:	Do you think that all skills can be taught or are some people born with them? Who do you think should pay for workers to acquire the skills they need – the employer or the worker? Do you think knowledge and qualifications are more important than experience when applying for a job? Some people think that professional people such as lawyers and doctors earn too much money. What's your opinion? How important is it to take enough time to spend time on hobbies? Some people think that practical manual skills will no longer be useful in 50 years' time. How far do you agree? Thank you. That is the end of the test.

Think about it
Reading and Use of English Part 1

1	FALSE	5	TRUE	9	TRUE
2	TRUE	6	TRUE	10	TRUE
3	TRUE	7	TRUE		
4	FALSE	8	FALSE		

Reading and Use of English Part 2

1
1	OF	6	OR
2	ONE/GAP/ITEM	7	ALWAYS
3	ONLY/JUST/DOWN	8	CASES/INSTANCES/ EXAMPLES/ITEMS
4	ARE	9	THIS/THAT
5	AS	10	ALL/OTHER

Reading and Use of English Part 3

1	it	7	end
2	one word	8	start
3	an	9	end
4	8	10	CAPITAL
5	word	11	carefully
6	is		

Reading and Use of English Part 4

1 c 2 f 3 a 4 e 5 h 6 b 7 d 8 g

Reading and Use of English Part 5

1 FALSE – There are four options: A, B, C or D.
2 TRUE
3 TRUE
4 FALSE – They are between 650 and 750 words.
5 TRUE
6 FALSE – This is done in Part 7 of the test.
7 TRUE
8 FALSE – The first three sources are possible, but texts are non-technical so are unlikely to come from specialist journals.

Reading and Use of English Part 6

1 f 2 d 3 a 4 h 5 b 6 c 7 e 8 g

Reading and Use of English Part 7

1 FALSE – six paragraphs are removed, which means that the main text probably has more than six paragraphs.
2 FALSE – they can come from a wide range of sources and are not limited to articles and reviews (although articles in particular are a very common text type).
3 TRUE
4 TRUE – it would be a bit easy if they weren't!
5 FALSE – there is only one extra paragraph.
6 TRUE
7 FALSE – only one of them can be a long single sentence. The others are multiple sentences.
8 FALSE – the missing paragraphs make up 40% of the total word count, which is between 650 and 800 words.

Reading and Use of English Part 8

1	multiple matching	5	extracts
2	section	6	the letter
3	four to six	7	ten questions
4	Part 6	8	between 600 and 700 words

Writing Part 1

1 c 2 d 3 b 4 f 5 a 6 e

Writing Part 2

1
1	2 3	3 220	4 260

Text types which would NOT appear in Advanced Writing Part 2: an article, an essay, a story

5	a report	6	a proposal
7	a review	8	an email/letter

Listening Part 1

1 three
2 multiple-choice
3 total
4 dialogue
5 topics
6 detail
7 agree
8 purpose
9 attitudes

Listening Part 2

1 monologue
2 talk
3 audience
4 style
5 specific
6 gap
7 order
8 phrase
9 spelling

Listening Part 3

1 two
2 discussing
3 interviewer
4 three to four
5 six
6 options
7 order
8 detailed
9 feelings
10 agree
11 purpose
12 read

Listening Part 4

1 theme
2 speaker
3 choose
4 match
5 extra
6 use
7 twice
8 order

Speaking Part 1

Good advice: 4, 6, 8
Not good advice:
1 A short pause is natural, but you should give prompt answers to the questions.

2 Give appropriate length answers to the questions, explaining your answers and giving reasons and examples. However, you should avoid giving overlong answers or dominating the conversation.
3 Pre-prepared answers are easily spotted and may not be appropriate answers to the questions asked.
5 In this part, you should direct your answer to the examiner who has asked you the question. You can, if appropriate, show that you have been listening to the other candidate(s) by relating your answer to theirs. (e.g. Like Johann, I enjoy skiing. As Mikaela said, …)
7 You should try to use a range of structures and lexis. At this level, examiners are looking for more complex language. It is likely that you will make more mistakes with this than with simpler language, so do not worry about this.

Speaking Part 2

1 b 2 c 3 a 4 e 5 d 6 g 7 f

Speaking Parts 3 & 4

1 telling
2 explaining
3 handing
4 look
5 tells
6 discussed
7 make
8 broaden
9 focus
10 develop

ACKNOWLEDGEMENTS

The authors and publishers acknowledge the following sources of copyright material and are grateful for the permissions granted. While every effort has been made, it has not always been possible to identify the sources of all the material used, or to trace all copyright holders. If any omissions are brought to our notice, we will be happy to include the appropriate acknowledgements on reprinting and in the next update to the digital edition, as applicable.

Text

Guardian News and Media Limited for the text on p. 36 adapted from 'Knowing the Score by David Papineau review – sport meets philosophy' by William Skidelsky, *The Guardian*, 26.05.2017. Copyright © 2017 Guardian News and Media Limited. Reproduced with permission; Guardian News and Media Limited for the text on pp. 48–49 adapted from 'Meet the nine billion-dollar companies turning a profit from sustainability' by Freya Williams, *The Guardian*, 02.01.2016. Copyright © 2016 Guardian News and Media Limited. Reproduced with permission; Guardian News and Media Limited for the text on pp. 52–53 adapted from 'Squeezing out arts for more 'useful' subjects will impoverish us all' by Stephanie Merritt, *The Guardian*, 26.06.2016. Copyright © 2016 Guardian News and Media Limited. Reproduced with permission.

Photographs

All the photographs are sourced from GettyImages.

p. 13: Pacific Press/LightRocket; p. 14: VisitBritain/Rod Edwards; p. 17: seb_ra/iStock/Getty Images Plus; p. 19: NoDerog/E+; p. 20: Pere Soler/Moment; p. 23: martinhosmart/iStock/Getty Images Plus; p. 24: barsik/iStock/Getty Images Plus; p. 26: asiseeit/E+; p. 29, 83, 100: Hero Images; p. 30, 62: Rawpixel/iStock/Getty Images Plus; p. 33: Westend61; p. 34: Athit Perawongmetha/Moment; p. 42: Johner Images; p. 45: piccaya/iStock Editorial/Getty Images Plus; p. 48: ilyast/DigitalVision Vectors; p. 52, 107 (photo 3), 109 (photo 4): Hill Street Studios/Blend Images; p. 54: skynesher/E+; p. 60: GrigoryLugovoy/iStock/Getty Images Plus; p. 64: Caiaimage/Martin Barraud/OJO+; p. 66: clu/iStock/Getty Images Plus; p. 68: Thomas Trutschel/Photothek; p. 71: Massonstock/iStock/Getty Images Plus; p. 72: Jordan Siemens/DigitalVision; p. 75: Savushkin/iStock/Getty Images Plus; p. 79: Andrew Peacock/Lonely Planet Images; p. 80: Cultura RM Exclusive/Jason Butcher/; p. 85: Edward Langley/Moment; p. 87: Cultura RM Exclusive/Stefano Gilera; p. 90: KrulUA/iStock/Getty Images Plus; p. 93: Holcy/iStock/Getty Images Plus; p. 95: HAYKIRDI/E+; p. 97: Jeff J Mitchell/Getty Images News; p. 99: sturti/E+; p. 102: David Malan/Photodisc; p. 105 (photo 1): FatCamera/E+; p. 105 (photo 2): svetikd/E+; p. 105 (photo 3): kali9/E+; p. 105 (photo 4): LeeTorrens/iStock/Getty Images Plus; p. 105 (photo 5): Matt Cardy/Getty Images News; p. 105 (photo 6): Bigshots/DigitalVision; p. 107 (photo 1): PeopleImages/E+; p. 107 (photo 2): Peter Langer/Perspectives; p. 107 (photo 4): Peter Cade/Iconica; p. 107 (photo 5): PeopleImages/DigitalVision; p. 107 (photo 6): Antonio_Diaz/iStock/Getty Images Plus; p. 108: Catherine Delahaye/Taxi; p. 109 (photo 1): Ashley Cooper/Corbis Documentary; p. 109 (photo 2): stevecoleimages/E+; p. 109 (photo 3): Greg Ceo/Photodisc; p. 109 (photo 5): Blend Images - Jose Luis Pelaez Inc/Brand X Pictures; p. 109 (photo 6): Laurence Monneret/Stockbyte; p. 111: Alistair Berg/DigitalVision; p. 112: AndrewJShearer/iStock/Getty Images Plus; p. 114: Peter Cade/The Image Bank.

The publishers are grateful to the following contributors: layout QBS Learning; audio recordings by DN and AE Strauss Ltd; Engineer: Neil Rogers; Editor: James Miller; Producer: Dan Strauss. Recorded at Half Ton Studios, Cambridge.